EVALUATING EDUCATIONAL INNOVATION

CROOM HELM EDUCATIONAL MANAGEMENT SERIES
Edited by Cyril Poster

Evaluating Educational Innovation

SHIRLEY HORD

CROOM HELM
London • New York • Sydney

© 1987 Shirley Hord
Croom Helm Ltd, Provident House, Burrell Row,
Beckenham, Kent, BR3 1AT
Croom Helm Australia, 44-50 Waterloo Road,
North Ryde, 2113, New South Wales

Published in the USA by
Croom Helm
in association with Methuen, Inc.
29 West 35th Street
New York, NY 10001

British Library Cataloguing in Publication Data

Hord, Shirley
    Evaluating educational innovation. —
    (Croom Helm education management series).
    Educational innovations
    I. Title
    379.1′54   LB1027
    ISBN 0-7099-4703-8

Library of Congress Cataloging-in-Publication Data

Hord, Shirley, M.
    Evaluating educational innovation.

    Includes bibliographies and index.
    1. Educational innovations — Evaluation. 2. School
improvement programs — Evaluation. I. Title.
LB1027.3.H67   1987   371.3′07′8   87-15706
ISBN 0-7099-4703-8

Printed and bound in Great Britain
by Billing & Sons Limited, Worcester.

FOREWORD

It is a personal as well as a professional pleasure to welcome this book into the Croom Helm education management series. I first met its author at an international conference on school improvement and I was much impressed by the work that she and her colleagues at the University of Texas at Austin had done over a long period to develop the Concerns Based Adoption Model for the evaluation of innovation. A few months later I was to experience Texas hospitality and a gruelling but enjoyable one to one tuition into the mysteries of the CBAM over a three day period. That tuition has been renewed and intensified a number of times since, in workshops, conversation and correspondence. I have come to consider CBAM a valuable instrument of worldwide validity and importance, and I hope that the publication of this book will considerably extend an understanding of its potential.

This volume is, however, much more than an account of an evaluation tool. Shirley Hord has contextualised all description of the model itself within a broad study of the evolution and rapid growth of curriculum innovation on both sides of the Atlantic. Furthermore, the book contains also a critical appraisal of both the practice and the literature of innovation and its evaluation — or, often, the lack of it. The rate of increase in innovatory practices in education in the United Kingdom has become a matter of great concern for most practitioners of education, and one begins to hear faint cries of 'Stop the world! I want to get off!' It is likely that this momentum will be maintained worldwide in the foreseeable future, as we learn to harness new technology to old skills. To have a better understanding of monitoring and evaluative procedures and skills is a vital strategy for coping, even for survival. This book contributes much to that understanding.

Cyril Poster

To

Frances and Beulah

Gene and Joe

CONTENTS

FIGURES

PREFACE

Educational innovation has been a persistent and ubiquitous feature of schooling in many countries during the last quarter century. Specific innovations have been developed to address virtually every conceivable educational concern, and substantial amounts of money and effort have been devoted to their introduction into schools. In the United States, in particular, a dizzying array of changes great and small has been almost continuously forthcoming for the past two decades. In many schools, a number of change efforts may well be taking place at the same time and most schools have averaged at least one innovation per year (Rutherford & Murphy, 1985). A school inspector of a large English LEA listed for the National Development Centre for School Management Training thirty-eight areas of change affecting schools, of which a substantial number were significant innovations; and further investigation revealed that a large secondary school might well be involved with from twelve to sixteen of them.

It does not require a great act of imagination to perceive the tremendous potential for disruption inherent in such undertakings, and certainly most educators, whether teachers, school leaders, or LEA personnel, could readily foresee at least some of the problems schools might expect to encounter in the course of their attempts to change and thereby improve themselves. It seems only fair, then, to consider what benefits are likely to accrue as a result of these innovations. Unfortunately, the answer to this question is neither simple nor spontaneous.

Innovations are of two kinds. On the one hand, there are new areas of learning within the curriculum, such as micro-electronics; new systems of examining, such as GCSE, and of recording: profiling, for example. On the other hand, there are alternatives to existing practices, such as the Schools Council Integrated Science Project (SCISP), Active Tutorial Work (ATW) or team teaching. In the past, there has been an unfortunate tendency to reject innovations before their effectiveness has been properly evaluated and to move on to their successors as quickly as they could be generated. Indeed, in the period in question, whole cycles of action and reaction, of unbounded enthusiasm for innovation followed predictably by an equally excessive disillusionment with and distrust of it, have been enacted in social as well as educational arenas. As we shall discover in subsequent chapters, the recent history of educational innovation is, like all history, a staggering amalgam of great ideas, bright moments, missed opportunities and tragic blunders. Happily though, and despite the inevitable turmoil, many of the best ideas have survived and even been improved by their time in the crucible; and equally importantly, from some of the mis-steps have come the beginnings of wisdom. We now know a great deal more about educational innovation than ever before.

Earlier innovations, though often generously funded and vigorously supported, commonly suffered from a woeful lack of attention. Planners and practitioners alike typically gave inadequate attention to the actual process of utilising the new programmes or products and integrating them into existing educational practice. This in turn stemmed from a lack of coherent, practical information about the process of educational change, which tended either to be seen as a 'given' that would automatically and swiftly follow the formal adoption of an innovation by a school, or else not to be seen at all. As we shall see, however, the demands for accountability that inevitably followed in the wake of massive expenditures of public funds, and the sometimes disquieting results of early attempts to evaluate innovations in progress, together provided a major stimulus to educational research. The result has been a steadily growing number of studies of the process of educational change and an increased knowledge base. From that knowledge and research, new understandings about the change process have developed, which have led in turn to new tools, procedures and techniques, battle tested, that can assist practitioners in introducing and guiding change.

This book is designed to present these vital tools to practitioners; accordingly, its approach is essentially pragmatic. Though firmly grounded in careful research, the information contained herein is practical and immediately applicable to real-life educational improvement efforts in schools. Concepts and measures for assessing, for monitoring and facilitating and for evaluating innovation use constitute the core of the book. They are presented in a sufficiently straightforward manner, it is hoped, to enable interested practitioners to gain immediate and lasting benefit in terms of their daily work.

It should be stressed that this is not a book about specific innovations. In these pages, the reader will find no elaborately outlined prescriptions for improving student achievement test scores in mathematics, say, or enabling students to attain great oracy in modern languages. Useful, innovative programmes of this sort already exist and, as already suggested, simple adoption of an innovation, however well planned, does not guarantee that positive results will accrue. Rather, this is a book about what to do with whatever innovation any school might have in mind: how to gauge the success of an innovation in progress, and what steps to take to maximise the prospects for full implementation and, therefore, optimal benefit. As such, its applicability transcends narrow categories, encompassing a wide variety of situations and contexts. For school leaders and other administrators, certainly, it is at least as important to understand the process of change and how it works as to have grasped all the minute particulars of the specific innovation they are seeking to introduce. For teachers using the innovation, who of course must have a thorough understanding of the programme if they are to impart it successfully to students, this additional knowledge can prove invaluable in helping them meet the challenges that change inevitably brings.

As already indicated, this book is primarily addressed to practitioners: the primary school curriculum coordinator, the secondary school head of department or faculty, the senior management team, the headteacher, the LEA adviser and inspector, the Chief Education Officer. It is not addressed to the researcher and the university don, though they will also find much that is of interest here. The sources for the material presented here are varied, representing the rich blend of perspectives and approaches the author has evolved over many years of work in the field. Hard data gleaned from research in schools is blended with informal and formal observations derived from clinical work and with judgments shaped by interactions with practitioners and theorists alike. I believe that informed clinical judgments as well as empirical research can produce a sound data base. Further, a combination of quantitative and qualitative data, of statistical measures and ethnographic procedures, can together provide a more complete and better balanced understanding of educational problems and practices than any single measure or approach. It is this multifaceted approach, then, that I wish to share with practitioner colleagues and all others interested in educational innovation.

At this point, some clarification of terms and meanings may be appropriate. To begin with, when we speak of innovation, it is in terms at once both broad and narrow: broad in their overall applicability and narrow in their specific point of reference. Innovation, as used in these pages, can refer to anything that is new to an individual within the system; and what is an innovation to one person may not be to another in the same school. Thus, innovations can include not only curricular changes but also new processes, products, ideas or even people. New attendance procedures, new textbooks or even a new principal might all be legitimately viewed as educational innovations.

Having said this, we may refer back to the title of this volume, <u>Evaluating Educational Innovation</u>, and consider more explicitly what that might mean. Obviously, based on our concept of innovation, evaluation must be approached with sufficient flexibility to admit the wide range of possibilities for subject matter. Evaluation in its more rigid context might not seem readily applicable to some less structured forms of innovation: ideas, for example. And certainly an appropriate evaluation system for textbooks might not appear transferable to head teachers and principals or vice versa! It is important to remember, though, that what we are really discussing when we speak of schools is people: students and teachers, heads and school inspectors. On this most basic and most often ignored or underrated level, the selfsame concept of evaluation may comfortably address the unlikeliest assortment of innovations. For, regardless of the nature of the change, it is people who will be using it, or refusing to do so, and responding to it in a variety of ways which may vitally affect both the manner and degree of that use. Thus, an understanding of the complex interactions between an innovation, its users and its targeted audience can be an invaluable aid to the practitioner in determining what exactly is happening with the new programme or product in the school and what, if anything, needs to be done about it.

Evaluation, in this sense, is not merely judgmental. As we shall discover in the chapters that follow, the concrete evaluation techniques that are described in these pages start from the premise that change is a process, that it happens over time, and usually a considerable period of time, and that different individuals within a school or system respond to it in different ways and adjust to it at their own pace. It is therefore inevitable, and quite natural, that certain individuals will have more trouble adapting to an innovation than others and may as a result offer more resistance to it. For the school leader or management team whose task it is to guide the course and pace of change, this means that different responses to different individuals, based on a clear understanding of their respective feelings and positions in regard to the innovation, will be not only appropriate but absolutely essential to successful implementation. Seen in this light, evaluating innovations is not a passive but an active task, and one that is as much forward-looking as present-directed. It is, in short, a principal component in the practitioner's kit bag for facilitating change.

In addressing the complex and delicate matter of educational change, then, the present volume must touch on a number of related issues. To do this, I have developed a tripartite structure that attempts to lead the reader logically and systematically through the appropriate steps, supplying background information as deemed necessary, and moving from a general picture to an increasingly detailed explication. For those readers who like to have some idea of where they're going in advance, however, as well as those who prefer to 'skip and sample', a brief word about the chapters and their respective contents may be helpful.

OVERVIEW OF BOOK

Part One, Surveying the Field, is an attempt to provide the reader with at least some sense of context. Information of whatever sort does not simply drop out of the sky; it has a history and a web of relations to the people and things it attempts to interpret or explain. Understanding something of these connections is, I believe, essential to a full apprehension of the meaning and significance of the subject matter. Accordingly, in Chapter One, I begin with an overview of the history of educational change during the last several decades, considering its sources, major influences and results. The oft-repeated wisdom about 'learning from the past' may have some relevance here; in any case, the beliefs, mistakes and intent of both prior change research and actual innovation programmes have left a major imprint on both the substance and direction of contemporary efforts, and thus may be of immediate interest to practitioners as aids to understanding the current scene.

In Chapter Two, I venture into the theoretical realm, looking at the various components of change that researchers have identified, and surveying representative samples of the best known, most influential change models. As with our historical survey, this one is necessarily abbreviated, but it does convey an idea of the broad range of general approaches to the question of what change is. Lest pragmatic readers flinch at the mere mention of the word 'theoretical', let me remind them that our goal, here as elsewhere, is to promote better practical understanding. Thus, by providing a vocabulary and suggesting some possibilities for kinds of change, knowledge of these components and models can help practitioners grasp what is going on in their schools, or what is likely to occur as they begin to implement an innovation. In addition, our discussion of the particular shortcomings of the various models suggests some of the fundamental conceptual and practical problems that are inevitably connected with the adoption and implementation of change in schools.

Chapter Three rounds out the ground-laying activities with a more overtly practitioner-oriented perspective. Instead of the abstract formulations of researchers and theoreticians, the positions presented here are more likely to have been distilled from the actual experiences of people in the school and in the classroom, though with additional analytical and interpretive input from researchers, of course. Viewing change as a process unfolding over time that passes through recognisable phases or subprocesses en route, this chapter provides a more precise means of pinpointing where along the time continuum we are with a particular innovation effort. It also gives a more detailed, pragmatic picture of what the change process actually looks like in schools.

Part Two, Tools For Change, comprises the core of the book. Having considered the mistakes of the past and the problems of the present, I now proceed to offer some concrete, practical solutions. The Concerns-Based Adoption Model (CBAM), consists of a set of interlocking, complementary techniques or procedures for evaluating change. Each of them might be visualised as a filter or lens with which certain vital information about the current status and pressing needs of a change in progress can be gleaned. Together, they provide a comprehensive, multidimensional picture of an innovation effort.

Chapter Four describes the three diagnostic dimensions of CBAM, which enable the head or other change facilitator to pinpoint precisely what is happening with an innovation in terms of the concerns and behaviours of individual teachers and, by extension, in the school as a whole. In Chapter Five, the two prescriptive dimensions of CBAM are explored, that is, those that focus on the specific actions taken by the head or facilitator in support of change. These enable facilitators both to plan their approach to an innovation effort, including the specific steps they will take to encourage and support the change, and to keep a detailed and accurate record of what they have done, as an aid to understanding what is going on and deciding what to do next. In both these chapters and for each CBAM dimension presented, specific, practical applications to planning, initiation, implementation and analytical reporting are discussed. Chapter Five, in addition, briefly treats questions of context and the concept of the management team. Thus, these two chapters provide a concise, concrete practitioner's guide to the intricacies of educational innovation, its promotion and management.

Part Three, Summing Up, does exactly what its title says. The major points covered in the previous chapters are reiterated in Chapter Six, helping the reader to focus on the most important messages. I have also attempted to anticipate and head off some possible areas of confusion or disagreement by clarifying a number of basic positions. To accomplish this, I describe several possible positions that I am not espousing, but that may inadvertently have been implied or suggested to the reader. I conclude with a note to educational researchers and policymakers suggesting how the material contained in the earlier chapters might apply to them.

In keeping with the earlier assertion that the book is addressed primarily to practitioners, rather than a more determinedly scholarly audience, I have tried to keep the text as straightforward and uncluttered as possible, holding references to a minimum. With regard to the references and examples that are cited, it might seem as though I have a bias toward North American sources. This is not chauvinism. Glatter (1986) readily acknowledges that 'the concept of school improvement is North American in origin' and, citing Clark, Lotto & Astuto (1984), 'that an impressive range of relevant empirical research has been conducted [in the US] and that there has been valuable and promising conceptual development.' By contrast, he finds European work in this field 'sparse', citing that of Hopkins and Wideen (1984) as a rare example.

This discrepancy notwithstanding, increasing attention is being focused on educational innovation, its meaning and its management, throughout the industrial world and, in fact, this lopsided state of affairs vis-a-vis research is already beginning to be rectified. The International School Improvement Project (ISIP), a sponsored project of the Organization for Economic Cooperation and Development/Centre for Educational Research and Innovation, is one promising example. Comprising educational researchers and practitioners from more than a dozen nations on three continents, ISIP addresses many facets of school change through its various area groups, drawing on the experiences of many countries to produce a truly international, cross-cultural perspective on common needs and common problems. Indeed, one of the most striking aspects of ISIP's ongoing work has been the repeated revelation of the extent to which the basic similarities in educational concerns cut across national and cultural lines, despite seemingly irreconcilable differences in outlook, methodology and system design.

Nowhere is this more apparent than between the United States and United Kingdom. Sir Keith Joseph, in his 1984 Sheffield speech, enumerated educational goals for England and Wales that are synonymous with those being widely proclaimed in the US. These include:

The need for minimum level curricular objectives to reduce gaps and overlaps (in Sir
Keith's words 'much of what many pupils are now
asked to learn is clutter.');

The need for more efficient use of resources in
a time of decreased funding;

The need for schools to play a greater role in
the transmission of ethical values;

The need for new insights in the selection and
appointment of head teachers, and for a generally higher quality teaching force (Joseph,
1984).

Significantly, even Sir Keith's critics and reactors
generally agreed with this assessment of needs
(Brighouse, 1984; Judge, 1984; Radice, 1984; Wilson,
1984). Thus, despite considerable historical and
cultural differences, some of which will be touched
on in the following chapters, both countries appear
to have arrived at very nearly the same place. This
consistent sympathy of needs and views has streng-
thened my conviction that the broad applicability of
the methods and perspectives presented here transcends the particularities of national practice or
belief.

ACKNOWLEDGEMENTS

Besides active participation in ISIP as a member of
Area Group Two, Principals and Internal Change
Agents in the School Improvement Process, I have
been privileged to interact with many well informed
and experienced colleagues in diverse areas of
education through my work at the Research and
Development Center for Teacher Education at The
University of Texas at Austin. My extensive travels
and simultaneous involvement in educational research
and practice have contributed significantly to the
evolution of the ideas presented here. In addition,
I have been encouraged by the series editor's
explicit instructions to 'say clearly what you
think, and why'; this book is the end product of a
lot of experience, thought and active involvement in
education. Ultimately, though, it remains very much
one person's viewpoint and is neither intended nor
presented as the last word on the subject of innovation. Were such epochal lines ever penned, we might

all well put aside our labours, for the millennium would be at hand. In the interim, however, this book is offered, with conviction and with hope, as a useful contribution to the continuing evolution of better educational systems.

I should be very quick to point out that Part Two of this book is an attempt to represent clearly and well some of the work done by my colleagues and myself at the Research and Development Center. For a dozen years, a team of researchers whose membership remained for the most part intact, an astonishing feat in and of itself, worked on broad-based and intensive longitudinal studies of organisational change, school improvement processes and the roles of leadership that initiate and support such endeavours. To the central members of this team, I owe a large measure of gratitude for the personal support and professional growth and productivity I have gained as their colleague. I salute Archie George, Gene Hall, Leslie Huling-Austin, Susan Loucks-Horsely, Beulah Newlove and Bill Rutherford. Other persons, more peripheral and in some cases less permanent, have contributed in a variety of significant ways to the work that has been developed and to my own possibilities to contribute to it: Oliver Bown, Marcia Goldstein-Toprak, Teresa Griffin, Suzanne Stiegelbauer, Joseph Vaughan and Patricia Zigarmi. It is necessary also to recognise Marge Melle, Harold Pratt and John Thurber, all school practitioners who have been our valued colleagues 'in the field', collaborating in the design and conduct of our studies of schools. Providing their technological expertise to shape this text to publication guidelines has been the considerable contribution of Elia Mar Diaz-Ortiz and Antoinette Rhodes and I thank them most abundantly. Last, this volume could not have happened had it not been for the patience, persistence and capable talents that Peter Gregutt, staff editor, contributed: to him, I am deeply indebted.

Finally, my participation in the Educational Management Series has been a valuable experience and very meaningful, made so by the gracious and generous roles that Cyril Poster, series editor, has played in the development of this manuscript: critical colleague, collegial critic. I am profoundly grateful.

REFERENCES

Brighouse, T. (1984). Comments on Sir Keith Joseph's speech. Oxford Review of Education, 10 (2), 151-154.

Clark, D.L., Lotto, L.S., & Astuto, T.A. (1984). Effective schools and school improvement: A comparative analysis of two lines of enquiry. Educational Administration Quarterly, 20 (3), 41-68.

Glatter, R. (1986). The management of school improvement. In E. Hoyle and A. McMahon (Eds.) World yearbook of education, 1986: The management of schools. London: Kogan Page.

Hopkins, D., & Wideen, M. (1984). Alternative perspectives on school improvement. London: Falmer Press.

Joseph, K., Sir. (1984). Speech by the Rt Hon Sir Keith Joseph, Secretary of State of Education and Science, at the North of England Education Conference, Sheffield, on Friday 6 January 1984. Oxford Review of Education, 10 (2), 137-148.

Judge, H. (1984). Comments on Sir Keith Joseph's speech. Oxford Review of Education, 10 (2), 154-156.

Radice, G. (1984). Comments on Sir Keith Joseph's speech. Oxford Review of Education, 10 (2), 149-151.

Rutherford, W.L., & Murphy, S.C. (1985). Change in high schools: Roles and reactions of teachers. Austin: Research and Development Center for Teacher Education, The University of Texas at Austin.

Wilson, J. (1984). Comments on Sir Keith Joseph's speech. Oxford Review of Education, 10 (2), 157-158.

Note to the Reader:
References published by the Research and Development Center for Teacher Education are available from the Southwest Educational Development Laboratory, 211 East Seventh Street, Austin, Texas, 78701, U.S.A.

Part One

SURVEYING THE FIELD

Chapter 1

THE FLOWERING OF INNOVATION: BLOSSOMS AND THORNS

In recent years, innovation has become a familiar
feature of the educational landscape, to the point
that younger people might readily assume that such
ubiquitous and frequent change was always a part of
the education scene. Nothing, however, could be
further from the truth. Education, like virtually
all other areas of human endeavour, appears to
follow a cyclical pattern, in which periods of
feverish activity give way to more tranquil intervals, which then eventually give rise to yet
another round of 'busy-ness'. At least in part,
this may be due to an inherent constitutional or
emotional inability to sustain such frenzied energies, not to mention the added stress and uncertainty that comes with change for too long, leading
the harried system- to disengage itself in order to
inaugurate the necessary conditions for recharging
the psychic and physical batteries.
     During the period in question, however, this
characteristic pattern has been further complicated
by the dramatic and escalating increase in the pace
of change, which leaves people less and less time to
assimilate the changes, much less to recover from
them. This trend has doubtless helped to fuel the
widespread perception of stress as a primary characteristic of life in industrial societies. It has
also, at least within the educational arena, contributed significantly to the increasing difficulty
for practitioners and researchers alike in either
gaining or maintaining any viable, long-range
perspective on what is happening in schools today.
And lacking such perspective, we will be ill-
equipped to make the kinds of vital decisions a
flourishing educational and social future demands.
With this in mind, then, let us revisit some seminal

3

educational events as we attempt to identify the forces and ideas that have shaped our course.

THE HEYDAY OF CURRICULUM INNOVATION

The mid 1960s witnessed a tremendous upsurge in educational innovation. Change, it seems, was in the air in many countries and, almost without exception, industrial societies experienced prolonged and often violent upheavals that tore the existing social fabric and overturned established practices and patterns. Social problems were addressed with an intense enthusiasm and many new programmes were developed to rectify what were seen as major areas of concern. Amid such extensive social change, schools, which stand at the intersection of so many diverse social vectors, were naturally caught up in the rush to improve, becoming the recipients of an unprecedented volume and diversity of change attempts. Predictably, the timing and specific character of these events varied somewhat from country to country, according to the particulars of the local context. At the same time, there was a surprising degree of uniformity in the overall shape and direction of the greater changes taking place. Consequently, it is possible to generalise on the basis of selected examples, despite the inevitable national differences.

In the United States, the first clear mandate for sweeping educational innovation actually took shape in the mid 1950s, predating the later social turmoil by a decade or more. Spurred by Cold War political pressures and the beginnings of the technology explosion, the National Science Foundation, in partnership with leading scientists, psychologists and educators, began an ambitious reform movement intended to transform radically the teaching of science and mathematics in the schools. The objective went far beyond mere curriculum revision; it set out to alter fundamentally the approach to science instruction in a way that would bring it more in line with the realities of scientific work and the needs of both students and adults in a rapidly changing technological society. Instead of emphasising the acquisition of an existing body of knowledge <u>about</u> science, as was traditionally done, the new approach focused on <u>inquiry</u>, on the <u>discovery</u> of knowledge by students through experimentation. This would, it was believed, more adequately prepare them both to become good scientists and to live in a world in which new areas of knowledge were being opened up with stunning frequency, while hallowed 'truths' were being regularly superseded or disproved. It was also decided to shift the emphasis from preparing a few apt students for technical careers to promoting a more general science literacy, and thereby enabling everyone to function more effectively in a highly technological society.

To achieve these goals, a multiplicity of programmes and projects was initiated. The Physical Science Study Committee (PSSC), founded by Zacharias in 1956 with a group of concerned university scientists, was an attempt to upgrade and modernise the high school science curriculum (Atkin & House, 1981). Similarly, other educational and professional groups designed new programmes, wrote new textbooks or organised symposia. The key to this sudden and abundant flowering of educational innovation was funding, provided in generous and steadily increasing amounts by the federal government, via the National Science Foundation, through the mid 1970s. It was, in fact, the largest governmental intervention in school science curricula in US history. Hundreds of millions of dollars in federal funds were earmarked for these programmes, which had also been widely acclaimed by leading scientists, educators and politicians. Partly because of its massive support and the momentum it generated, the movement began to spill over into other areas of education. Besides the sciences and mathematics, social studies and even English were affected by what was touted as a true educational revolution.

In the meantime a second major innovation wave, also funded by the federal government, was under way in American schools. The primary concern of this effort was educational equity: specifically, attending to the needs of educationally disadvantaged children, and attempting to insure them equal opportunities in education. The beginnings of this movement can be traced to the passage of the Elementary and Secondary Education Act (ESEA) in 1965. The backbone of that landmark act was Title I, which channelled funds to school districts, thus enabling them to provide special programmes for children from low-income families. Title I remained a major funding source for schools for many years and, as the drive for educational equality accelerated, a great many other federal programmes followed in its wake. One of the best known and most durable of these is Head Start, which attempts to undo the limiting effects of family poverty on a child's subsequent educational experience by introducing disadvantaged, preschool-aged children to many of the things their more fortunate peers would have absorbed or been exposed to at home, thereby bringing them all to a more equal level of capability by the time they begin conventional schooling. Other programmes addressed different aspects of the problem. And, in addition to these specific educational change efforts, dissemination programmes, such as the regional educational laboratories (also created by ESEA) and the National Diffusion Network, were initiated to help practitioners keep pace with the flood of new educational resources and practices theoretically available to them.

These latter programmes were, at least in part, an acknowledgement of some of the unforeseen problems brought on by the massive infusion of dollars, materials and special personnel into the schools. For, as with the introduction of inquiry teaching in science and mathematics, what began as a top-down legislative attempt at school improvement soon mushroomed as enthusiastic planners and legislators boldly took on such concerns as the disadvantaged learner, the special needs of talented and gifted students, bilingual education and the growing pressure to increase student freedoms and choices. Inevitably, this bewildering array of new demands and possibilities brought with it staggering logistical difficulties. In keeping with the mechanistic, development-oriented approach that spawned this flood of innovations, however, little or no provision had been made to anticipate or deal with the consequences. In retrospect, based on what we know now about educational innovation, what followed might seem to have been totally predictable. But at the time, amid that unprecedented flurry of rapid development, seemingly unlimited financial support and boundless enthusiasm, the real problems were not even suspected.

THE RISE OF ACCOUNTABILITY

As we have seen, one of the most distinguishing features of the American school improvement efforts of the 1960s and 70s was the large amount of public money allocated for their design and installation in the schools. Certainly, to the harried school leaders of today, who are continually being asked to do more with less, the prospect of virtually limitless funds must seem to border on the fabulous. But even this idyllic situation had its downside, the effects of which were not long in being felt. For with that generous financial support, or following swiftly in its wake, came demands for accountability.

Despite the lamentable ignorance of the process of educational change on the part of both planners and legislators, there was certainly no lack of awareness of the quantities of money being spent. Almost all of the innovative programmes that appeared during these years were dependent in one way or another on grants of monies, materials or other resources to schools. Naturally, those agencies providing the support wished to know what they were getting for their money and the awards were frequently accompanied by evaluation requirements. In itself, there is nothing inherently objectionable about the concept of accountability and it must have seemed eminently reasonable to those lawmakers who included this requirement in their reform bills. Yet the cumulative effects of these innocent attempts to ensure educational quality control were out of all proportion to their initiators' intent, so much so, in fact, that their impact is still being felt today.

The most immediate effect of the evaluation requirements on schools was to augment substantially what was already a logistical disaster. School leaders and teachers alike were overwhelmed by the additional demands on their time that responsible financial and logistical management of the new programmes required. For school leaders, in particular, simply completing the requisite paperwork and meeting the regulations for use of the resources in question took up so much of their time as virtually to ensure that they would be unable to serve as instructional leaders or otherwise assist in the implementation of innovations. And teachers, for their part, found themselves in the unenviable position of having not only to cope with the practical problems and accompanying anxieties that any new enterprise must bring, but also to wade through an adamantly unparted sea of paperwork and red tape, all in the absence of significant technical or emotional support. The upshot, for both school leaders and teachers, was more work, more pressure and more anxiety, without necessarily any corresponding increase in professional satisfaction. For, all too often, the actual innovations simply

7

got lost, drowned or smothered under a rising tide of frustrations.

A second, less immediately apparent effect of the evaluation requirements proved in the long run to be even more significant. By directing the attention of planners, practitioners and legislators to the demonstrable results of innovations, they helped initiate a fundamental shift in the whole process unfolding in the schools. The earlier change efforts, as we have seen, focused almost exclusively on development. New programmes, curricula and materials were designed, produced and delivered to the schools, with the assumption that all would then be well. Now, however, increasing emphasis began to be placed on outcomes and, consequently, the first clear indications of some of the hidden problems in the innovation process began to become apparent.

Apart from the immediate logistical difficulties imposed by evaluation requirements, there were several more fundamental problems that critically affected the results the requirements elicited. In the first place, the evaluations, as opposed to the actual programmes, were primarily political in nature. That is, they were intended to justify the considerable expenditure of public monies that the innovations entailed, and thereby to protect the programmes' sponsors from accusations of profligacy, preferably in time for the next election. This was not expected to cause undue problems, since those involved seemed confident that the results would amply meet their developers' rosy predictions. In practice, though, this usually meant that programme evaluations were required <u>much too soon</u> to show any definitive improvement: typically, only one or two years after programme introduction. Furthermore, the evaluation format used often failed to correspond adequately to the innovation in question, which inevitably led to serious discrepancies between what was being measured and reported on and what was actually happening in classrooms. In general, these problems with evaluations can be traced, in large measure, to a fundamental ignorance concerning the innovation process. For the most part, neither planners nor practitioners even recognised the existence of such a process; and, this being so, they could hardly be expected to show much in-depth understanding of it.

When the results of these required evaluations became available, then, they regularly failed to reveal any significant gains in student performance.

And the ripples set off by the steady accumulation of unfavourable data travelled far and wide. One immediate consequence was a dramatic increase in the amount of research being done on educational change, as a search of ERIC journal citations on the topic from 1969 through the early 1970s confirms (Firestone & Corbett, forthcoming). Faced with a seemingly objective denial of the programmes' effectiveness, researchers naturally began asking what was wrong. This research boom was also fuelled by a more widespread phenomenon which went beyond the boundaries of strictly educational concerns. Almost without exception, the sweeping social programmes of President Lyndon Johnson's Great Society were being criticised and their effectiveness challenged. Once begun, this questioning quickly attained the same momentum that had characterised the innovation wave that preceded it.

At the same time, there was another response to the largely negative evaluation results that seemed to work almost at cross-purposes to the main thrust of research. To the frustrations of school leaders and teachers were now added the frustrations of planners and policymakers, who found themselves called upon both to explain why their innovative programmes had failed to produce rapid, measurable gains in student performance and to figure out what to do about it. Faced with these pressures, the most common response was to say that the programme in question was at fault and to scrap it in favour of an even newer one. Given the widespread publicity attending the wholesale revision of the education system, in which the already loaded issue of public education was made even more controversial by the massive expenditure of public funds, such a hasty reaction was perhaps understandable. Unfortunately, it only served to increase still more the already rampant frustrations of practitioners, who now saw programmes they had struggled to assimilate blithely discarded as newer but equally problematic ones took their place. A regular cycle of adoption, evaluation, rejection and substitution evolved, as a practical corollary to the ongoing philosophical debate between those stressing curriculum development and those emphasising student outcomes. For teachers, though, who witnessed the annual arrival and demise of innovations, a kind of self-protective indifference took hold, as they developed a highly sceptical wait-and-see attitude toward anything new, based on the seemingly reasonable assumption that it, too, would soon be gone.

Researchers, meanwhile, continued to delve into the question of why these programmes were not delivering as expected. Through the 1970s, many case studies of specific innovations were conducted. Inevitably, the design and consequently the outcome of each one were to a significant degree functions of the investigators' concept of change. An evaluation of Head Start, for instance, focused on measurable changes in the IQs of children in the programme, paying little attention to its content or methodology. In this, the study mirrored the development-oriented model of change that had produced so many of the programmes to begin with. But since the change in children's IQs was less than expected, the questions still remained. Increasingly, then, researchers and policymakers began asking whether the programmes had in fact been implemented as originally planned.

This seemingly simple question quickly brought a major shift in the overall perspective on change in schools. Charters and Jones (1973) called attention to the tenuous nature of evaluations based on comparisons of experimental and control groups when it was not certain whether there had been any difference in the treatment the two groups received. Other researchers (Murphy, 1971; Pressman & Wildavsky, 1973) took issue with the basic mechanism of federal aid to education, arguing that political and logistical considerations fatally compromised the government's ability to ensure that its funds were put to their intended uses. Suddenly, the previous decade's most cherished assumptions were under attack; indeed, it almost seemed as though the whole complex edifice of innovation and evaluation had been built on shifting sands.

Meanwhile, more careful data continued to be collected, suggesting that the 'new, improved' programmes were not working as expected, either. Even when a considerable period of time was allowed for an innovation to take effect and extensive resources were devoted to analysis, the results often appeared to be negligible. In 1976, for example, the National Science Foundation commissioned a massive attempt to evaluate the results of its twenty years of sponsorship of reforms in the teaching of science, mathematics and social studies. Three major studies assessed the effects of this so-called educational revolution on actual classroom practice. In addition, ten interpretative studies analysed the resulting mountain of data from a variety of professional perspectives (Kyle, 1984).

Given all of this, the conclusions were indeed chastening. Among the studies' voluminous findings were the following (Stake & Easley, 1978):

1. In spite of massive infusion of money and effort, school science has not changed significantly during the last two decades. Instructional programmes designed in the 1960s and 1970s are not widely used in schools. Inquiry teaching is not occurring to any extent nor is inquiry an operational goal of science instruction in schools.

2. Although some students are receiving excellent science instruction, the majority of US school students are not receiving science instruction that is adequate for informed participation in our technological society.

3. Science instruction is largely text-centred and emphasis is placed on preparation of a small portion of students for careers in science and engineering; science for citizenship in a technological society receives little attention.

Obviously, things were not going as anticipated; something was wrong. And as the various programme evaluations and other research studies continued to be carried out, additional pieces of the puzzle gradually came to light. What they all seemed to point to was an almost total lack of understanding of what happens when an innovation is introduced into a school. Neither the developers who created the new programmes, nor the policymakers who supported them, nor the practitioners who bravely attempted to use them, nor the researchers who evaluated them and subsequently tried to discover what went wrong, had that understanding of the process of change that is essential to successful implementation.

Once this became apparent, however, appropriate responses could begin to be made. More and more educational research was undertaken that examined the process of change, as distinct from the problems and exigencies of a particular innovation. To spearhead this effort, one of the national educational research centres, The Research and Development Center for Teacher Education at The University of Texas at Austin, was assigned to investigate this broad-based educational concern. There, monitored by the National Institute of Education, a programme of research was developed to address vital questions about the improvement process in schools and colleges. Over a period of time, based on this work as well as other important research carried out at universities and research facilities across the country, a coherent, useful picture of the process of change, and its implications for educational innovators, began to coalesce.

THE HYPOTHESISED PROBLEM OF INNOVATION

Perhaps the greatest single failing of most educational change theory prior to 1970 and, consequently, of many of the change efforts developed from that research, was the reliance on an over simplistic model of change that could not begin to do justice to the complexities of the issue for schools. According to this view an innovation, once formally adopted, could automatically be considered 'in place' in daily practice in schools. That is, educational innovation was equated with the introduction of a new type of genetically engineered grain or some other strictly material innovation in a mechanistic, technical field. If the grain were planted and cared for according to directions, yields would measurably improve, a clear and objective correlation that no one could argue with. Education, however, is another matter altogether. Teacher/student relationships are infinitely more complex than those between a farmer and his seed corn and the social context of a classroom or a school is hardly comparable to that of a fresh-ploughed field. Unfortunately, these distinctions were not always made and, as we have seen, the effects of that lack of foresight were far reaching indeed.

Once researchers went beyond this tidy model, though, and began questioning their optimistic assumptions about change, their whole perception of the problem altered. For if new programmes were not being implemented as their developers intended, or were simply not being implemented at all, as was too often the case, the problem was not necessarily one of programme design and the wisest solution need not be automatically to scrap one programme and replace it with another, 'better' one. Instead, implementation began to be seen as perhaps the major problem in educational reform, and researchers, in their attempts to come to grips with this virtually unknown quantity, turned increasingly to other fields. The trend is clearly illustrated by one review of the relevant change literature for educators in the early 1970s (Giacquinta, 1973), in which only 47 of the 106 publications cited were unarguably from sources within the field of education. And this deliberate combing of other disciplines in search of applicable ideas, together with the previously noted substantial increase in educational change research overall, did eventually lead to the development of valuable new tools to aid practitioners in implementing innovations.

In the meantime, though, the self-perpetuating cycle of new programme development, evaluation, rejection and replacement was still very much in evidence. Faced with a growing body of evidence detailing the potential and actual problems connected with implementing educational innovations, a widespread attempt was made to sidestep neatly or simply circumvent these complications. In fact, one of the espoused objectives of many of the curriculum development groups of the sixties was to create curriculum innovations that would be essentially 'teacher-proof' in terms of their implementation in classrooms. This was in complete opposition to earlier practice. Prior to the launching of Sputnik in 1957, which symbolically signalled the beginning of the period discussed in this chapter, decisions about teaching and curriculum were almost exclusively in the hands of teachers at the local level and curriculum materials were synonymous with textbooks. But with the subsequent drive to modernise and redirect the educational system, responsibility for the design and development of curriculum was transferred to national curriculum development groups.

This centralisation of curriculum development as a vehicle for widespread educational change epitomised the 'top-down' approach to innovation. Generally speaking, change can occur in two very different ways in schools. It may be imposed from the top down, a strategy typically used by regional and national agencies to encourage more change more rapidly. Conversely, change can also evolve from the bottom up. In the latter case, a single teacher, a group of teachers or even an entire school works to identify existing problems or potential areas of improvement within the school, generate solutions and put them into practice. Either of these approaches can be used to produce significant, positive change in schools; at the same time neither one, in and of itself, provides any guarantee that useful results will be obtained. The key to successful innovation is implementation; and the unwritten rules of implementation remain the same, whether approached from above or below.

The attempts of the sixties developers to design teacher-proof curricula, then, were largely failures, not because they were for the most part imposed on schools from the top down but because they ignored some fundamental tenets of the process of change. In particular, they ignored or tried to bypass teachers and their crucial role with respect to any classroom innovation. As early as 1967 Gallagher, in the first of what was to become a series of classic studies of classroom implementation, hinted at the fallacy of the teacher-proof curriculum assertion. In his study of four high school teachers implementing the same innovative, inquiry-based science curriculum, Gallagher systematically documented that all of them had strikingly different patterns of practice in their classrooms, although they were using identical curriculum materials. During the 1970s, the notion that teachers' classroom practice could be quite different from the developer's intention, and that this had to be taken into consideration when an innovation was being planned and implemented, gradually gained currency.

One of the chief reasons for this was the considerable influence of the Rand Study of Federal Policies Supporting Educational Change (Berman & McLaughlin, 1975). Perhaps the most frequently cited study of the period, it critically affected the thinking of academics and policymakers alike. Based on a survey of 293 federally funded programmes as well as interviews with school superintendents, principals and teachers, and visits to 29 project sites, the Rand Study assessed different patterns of innovation adoption and use, and took a closer look at the problem of implementation. Three basic patterns of innovation use were distinguished: non-implementation, cooptation and mutual adaptation. In cooptation, the innovation was fundamentally altered to suit the local status quo; in mutual adaptation, both the innovation and the local setting were adjusted to produce a change that was in keeping with the spirit of the programme and also suited to the specifics of the local situation. The latter was identified as both the most desirable and least common approach. In fact, the study went further still, concluding that mutual adaptation was prerequisite to successful implementation, whereas the specifics of federal policies regarding change had relatively little effect.

The concept of mutual adaptation became the watchword of 1970s change research and, as a result, the central position of teachers in any model of school change was increasingly recognised. Most of the educational innovations attempted in all countries over the last several decades have had as their ultimate target the student: that is, they were intended in one way or another to have a beneficial influence on students and to improve the quality of their educational experience. But since students' educational experience is largely mediated by teachers it is they, in fact, who are usually the ones most affected by innovations, at least initially. A number of studies have confirmed the significant impact of change on the concerns of teachers (George & Rutherford, 1980; Hall, 1976; Hall & Rutherford, 1976). But as the Rand Study showed, this influence is mutual: teachers, in turn, represent a crucial link in any effort to change schools. Just as implementation may be conceived to be the fundamental central phase in the process of change, so teachers must be recognised as an irreducible middle component in implementation. In the words of one noted educational researcher, 'Educational change depends on what teachers do and think--it's as simple and complex as that' (Fullan, 1982, p. 107). This being so, the notion of a teacher-proof innovation may be conclusively rejected as an outright impossibility. In every country in the world, the student/teacher interaction is at the very core of the educational system, and is in fact the medium through which most transmission of knowledge takes place.

This conclusion, however, merely leads us to the next question: Teachers may be crucial to successful educational change, but what exactly is their role in it? For a variety of reasons, many educational innovations in schools are top-down changes: that is, they are 'handed down' to teachers from some outside source and teachers are then expected to make them work. Thus, despite their vital involvement in school change, teachers tend to be recipients rather than initiators of change. At this point, therefore, we must begin to look beyond the classroom, including in our consideration the whole local context: regional officers, external resource personnel and, in particular, principals or

headteachers. One of the most significant understandings to emerge from the cumulative body of
change research is the realisation that the individual school, the bottom line for the success or
failure of innovations, is a system, and no part of
it is separate from any other part. More than this,
it is a system comprised of people constantly
interacting in one way or another with one another.
Clearly then, whatever exerts the greatest influence
on the nature and course of those interactions will
be of vital importance to successful implementation;
and, as very strong and remarkably consistent
evidence suggests, the principal's actions or lack
of them may be the single most significant factor
affecting the success or failure of implementation
in a given school. Both through their direct
involvement with the innovation and their facilitation of teacher interaction and other key subprocesses, headteachers wield decisive influence in
determining whether or not implementation takes
place. In the following chapters, we will begin to
explore the conceptual and practical significance of
this great, and often unrealised, leadership potential.

CONCLUSION: WHERE YOU'VE BEEN DETERMINES
WHERE YOU GO

This chapter is essentially a historical overview of
the last several decades in educational innovation.
During this period, the UK and USA have followed
similar paths and, as mentioned earlier, have
arrived virtually at the same place in terms of
educational goals. This chapter of review is meant
to provide useful perspectives on what follows. To
this end, it has discussed the most widespread and
significant trends of the period, regardless of
their outcome. It may have seemed to some readers,
however, that unwarranted attention was being paid
to conceptual fallacies and mistaken or discredited
policies. But the painful truth is that the problems and mis-steps of the years in question constitute vital stages in the evolution of our understanding of the process of change in schools; useful
knowledge, as always, must be hard won. Moreover,
the recurring problems that plagued so many innovation efforts and defied the expectations of curriculum developers ultimately provided the major impetus
to change research that has led, in turn, to the

development of the invaluable knowledge base we have today.

Based on this collected body of data about specific innovations and what happened to them as they were introduced into schools, conceptual models of the process of educational change have been constructed. To the extent that these models accurately reflect real happenings in schools, they are valuable tools for practitioners involved in implementing an innovation at whatever level. By providing a general picture of what is or may be going on in a headteacher's school during implementation, an accurate change model can help clarify what the specific problems are, and what concrete actions can be taken to alleviate them. In the following chapter, therefore, I explore some of these change models and attempt to elucidate what each has to offer the practitioner.

REFERENCES

Atkin, J.M., & House, E.R. (1981). The federal role in curriculum development: 1950-1980. Educational Evaluation and Policy Analysis, 3 (5), 5-36.

Berman, P., & McLaughlin, M.W. (1975). Federal programs supporting educational change, Vol. IV: The findings in review. Santa Monica, CA: Rand Corporation.

Charters, W.W., & Jones, J.E. (1973). Barriers to the innovation process: Four case studies of differentiated staffing. Educational Administration Quarterly, 9 (1), 3-14.

Firestone, W.A., & Corbett, H.D. (forthcoming). Organizational change. In N. Boyan (Ed.) Handbook of research on educational administration. New York: Longman.

Fullan, M. (1982). The meaning of educational change. New York: Teachers College Press.

Gallagher, J. J. (1967). Teacher variation in concept presentation in BSCS curriculum programs. BSCS Newsletter, 30.

George, A., & Rutherford, W.L. (1980). Changes in concerns about the innovation related to adopter characteristics, training workshops, and the use of the innovations. Austin: Research and Development Center for Teacher Education, The University of Texas at Austin.

Giacquinta, J. (1973). The process of organiza-
tional change in schools. In F.N. Kerlinger
(Ed.) Review of research in education. Itasca,
IL: F.E. Peacock.

Hall, G.E. (1976). The study of individual teacher
and professor concerns about innovations.
Austin: Research and Development Center for
Teacher Education, The University of Texas at
Austin.

Hall, G.E., & Rutherford, W.L. (1976). Concerns of
teachers about implementing team teaching.
Austin: Research and Development Center for
Teacher Education, The University of Texas at
Austin.

Kyle, W.C., Jr. (1984). What became of the curriculum development projects of the 1960s? In D.
Holdzkom & P. Lutz (Eds.) Research within
reach: Science education. Charleston, West
Virginia: Appalachia Educational Laboratory.

Murphy, J.T. (1971). Title I of ESEA: The poli-
tics of implementing federal education reform.
Harvard Educational Review, 41 (1), 35-63.

Pressman, J.L., & Wildavsky, A. (1973). Implementation. Berkeley, CA: University of California Press.

Stake, R. E., & Easley, J. A., Jr. (1978). Case
studies in science education. Washington,
D.C.: U.S. Government Printing Office.

Chapter 2

WHAT IS THIS THING CALLED CHANGE?

Every culture builds on certain concepts, principles or values that are so fundamental as to be seemingly beyond question. They are the sacrosanct entities that underlie everything, the conceptual threads that hold the whole social fabric together. Freedom and justice are two common ones that come to mind and, certainly, there are numerous others. Together they constitute a significant part of the intellectual and ethical heritage of humankind. But their very universality sometimes seems to work against them, for no one, in practice, knows exactly what they are. By their very ubiquitousness and universally acknowledged value, they have been exempted from close scrutiny, as if out of fear that to admit any doubt about the identity or substance of such pillars of the social order were somehow to subvert it. Whatever the explanation, this kind of fundamental inquiry is seldom undertaken, and when and if it is, the usual result is a hasty retreat from questions of such ambiguous and problematic character.

To be sure, the Babylonian scribes who pressed their wedge-shaped styli into wet clay, recording Hammurabi's Code for the judgement of their fellows and the benefit of future generations, did their part in addressing the thorny subject of justice and there has been no shortage of subsequent attempts to codify the essence of a pure ideal. But these pragmatic efforts merely seek to specify the working out of that ideal, not its substance; for the most part, their chief accomplishment has been keeping legions of lawyers, politicians and preachers busy. Fortunately, one need not comprehend the farthest ramifications of what we call justice in order to produce laws and practices that at least aim at ensuring it.

21

What is This Thing Called Change?

Another hallowed concept with a pedigree at least as long is the idea of change. Heraclitus declared continual flux to be the ruling principle of all existence and, unknown to him, his intellectual and spiritual brethren in ancient China had already enshrined the same notion in the arcane syllogisms of the I Ching or Book of Changes and the pithy phrases of the Tao Te Ching. More recently, the concept of change, now inextricably linked with its Siamese twin, progress, has become a philosophical cornerstone of many industrial democracies, that see it as an almost automatic good, equating continual change with a seemingly inevitable progression toward perfection. Certainly these assumptions have been operant in the field of education, as we have already seen; and the immediate results of this simplistic worship of change for its own sake merely proved that our understanding of it was no clearer than our blurry conception of justice. Unlike the latter, however, educational innovation cannot be so successfully pursued on such a hazy basis; we need concrete, coherent plans, based on a thorough understanding of the nature of our objective.

Having learned these lessons, educational researchers increasingly began to zero in on their elusive quarry. From the growing numbers of detailed case studies of specific innovations, attempts were made to elucidate the underlying principles of change and thereby to construct a useful picture of the process which would help both to identify the problems with existing innovations and to avoid repeating them in the future. This recognition of change as a process emphasised the time element, triggering a search for ways to measure where along this time line a given innovation was. Attempts were made to identify the various components of change and to discover ways of talking about them. The complex evolution of change theory gave rise to the development of a specialised terminology and, thus, a convenient shorthand key to new understandings. I believe a reasonable grasp of basic terms helps to bridge the gap between theoretician and practitioner and also enables the reader better to make sense of what follows. Therefore, before we proceed to an examination of some influential models of change, we would do well to consider what have come to be regarded as basic components and to establish their meanings.

A GLOSSARY OF CHANGE COMPONENTS

Perhaps the most basic and, unfortunately, still the most common conception of change is to equate it with adoption of an innovation. As we saw in Chapter One, early change research tended, in a rather remarkable leap of faith or logic, to apply the results of studies of non-educational phenomena to the field of education. The principal problem was believed to be how to get innovations adopted; after that, it was thought, things would take care of themselves. Thus adoption was seen as a formal and rational decision to change. Over time, this initial conception did get subdivided into phases, from early awareness through an initial trial to, eventually, formal adoption. Interestingly, the notion of change as an unfolding, temporal process is implicit in this progression of phases. The recognition was there, but it simply was not extended far enough, because the vision of change as an implicitly mechanical, semi-automatic event was still too strong. Notwithstanding these limitations, however, adoption remains a vital component of change, particularly from an organisational viewpoint.

Closely related to adoption is diffusion and, at least through the late 1950s, the two of them together were believed to account for the whole process of change. Diffusion is the spread of awareness and use of an innovation; at some elusive but variously defined point, it more or less blends into adoption. Diffusion was commonly thought of as a natural process, a kind of ripple effect, which is perhaps why little effort was devoted to encouraging it. Eventually, it was thought, a 'good' or useful innovation would spread throughout the population of possible users; it was simply a question of how long this might take. Here again, the emphasis was on time, which was what diffusion studies looked at: in general terms, how long it would take for a new idea to spread throughout a given social system. The answer, not surprisingly, was 'Very long, indeed'. Paul Mort, in his studies of educational innovations, concluded that it took approximately 50 years for an innovation such as kindergarten to be adopted by 95 per cent of US school systems, purely on the basis of unassisted, natural diffusion (Mort, 1953). Waiting for diffusion, it seems, may be analogous to <u>Waiting for Godot</u>.

At this point in our survey of conceptual evolution, we have caught up to where we began in

23

the previous chapter: the late 1950s, when sweeping changes began to be introduced into schools nationwide. The postwar explosion in scientific knowledge and the attendant realisation that curricula and texts alike were seriously out of date prompted a clarion call for reform. Money was as abundant as optimism, and the result, as we have seen, was a headlong rush to develop new educational materials. Development, it was believed, was the answer. The idea was to bring in all the experts, including scientists, mathematicians and learning theorists, allot them ample resources and let them design the new textbooks, curricula and other innovative packages that were clearly needed in order to promote up-to-date, effective education. If this were done properly, including all the latest ideas about innovation and the most current content possible, it was believed that change, and instant change at that, would be inevitable. With so much going for it, how could change not happen? As we have seen, though, something was left out of all the careful calculations, for the highly touted, elaborately prepared innovations of the period did not, for the most part, live up to their makers' expectations. Development alone could not guarantee change. At worst, as the National Science Foundation studies showed (Stake & Easley, 1978), even painstakingly developed innovations simply languished, without ever having been put to use; at best, they were left to the ponderous mercies of natural diffusion, in which case, according to Mort's conclusions, we will still be a long time awaiting results.

The next step in this gradual progression of understanding was recognition of the need for dissemination. After the development craze had been in vogue for a while and innumerable innovations had been developed, adopted and then scrapped and replaced by even newer ones, the idea began to take hold that what was needed was not more development but better utilisation, or any utilisation at all, for that matter, of what we already had. Instead of relying on the vagaries of diffusion to foster the spread of innovations, developers began to consider dissemination as an organised, planned and actively prosecuted phase of the change process. To accomplish this, summer institutes were established specifically to train teachers in the use of the innovations that had been developed for them. In addition, special linking agents were designed to serve as intermediaries between teachers and developers. These external resource people, often working for such groups as the National Diffusion Network (NDN), the Research and Development Exchange (RDX) or other similar organisations, play an active part in the marketing of educational innovations to school systems.

The trouble with all of these concepts, however, is that they focus exclusively on the early phases of change; none of them look past the adoption point to see what actually happens to the innovation once it is in the school. In this, they still reflect the somewhat naive assumption of the early change researchers that adoption equals effective use of an innovation. More recently, though, another phase of crucial importance in the change process has attracted increasing attention. This is implementation which refers to the actual, regular and proper use of an innovation in the school. In other words, the fact that an innovation was developed, presented to a school system by dissemination personnel and formally adopted by a local school's council does not necessarily imply or ensure that it will actually be used by teachers in that school or school system. Or if it is, it may not be used in the intended manner. A whole complex web of interlocking factors comes into play here in determining whether or not implementation takes place and, if so, to what extent. Failure to recognise this has brought about the untimely demise of many promising innovations; thus, it is not surprising that so much emphasis has been placed on implementation in recent years. Understanding that there is such a thing as implementation and, further, that it is likely to unfold gradually over a period of years, are two critical steps on the road to successful innovation.

Even having come this far, though, there is still no guarantee that lasting change has been effected. The recent literature on change is rife with examples of innovations that were adopted, implemented and then simply abandoned a few years later. At least one additional phase of change must be recognised, therefore, in order to encompass the later stages of the innovation continuum. Implementation is usually concerned with the first few years of an innovation's lifespan in a school, during which time there may be available additional funds, support from external change facilitators and the encouragement and sanction of senior management or other educational authorities to use the innovation. But if it is truly to last, change must be

25

institutionalised: that is, fully incorporated into the organisational structure of the school. This means that when the special funds are no longer available, the external facilitators have gone, the attention of the LEA has turned to other problems and the headteacher leaves for another school, the innovation will remain, for it has been incorporated into daily practice on a routine level. Only then can we say that institutionalisation has taken place and conclude with some real confidence that lasting change has been effected.

These, then, are some of the major subsets of change that have come to be recognised. Naturally, not all researchers employ identical terminology or sequence; additionally, there may be other important components that have yet to be defined. But these subprocesses give us a broad conceptual picture of what we mean when we speak of the change process. Having clarified their meanings for the reader, we are now ready to begin applying them to specific models of change, in order to map out in greater detail what the likely course of an innovation's progress through the educational system may be.

A MODEST CHANGE TAXONOMY

If early change research shunned or simply over-looked the change process and the question of how it might look or behave in favour of more concrete, deterministic subjects, subsequent work has more than corrected the oversight. The last decade or so has seen the creation of many such conceptual models of change, covering a broad spectrum of possible approaches. The approach each writer or group of writers takes is, naturally, a function of their underlying assumptions; and these, particularly in regard to educational change, inevitably expose basic philosophical differences on the part of their authors.

The complex, thorny nature of educational innovation is due in no small measure to the identities of some of its principal components. To begin with, education itself is a wide-ranging field that necessarily involves itself with questions of fundamental ethical and social values. As such, it could scarcely hope to avoid serious and, at times, bitter controversy. Additionally, the chief actors in the educational arena are the vast numbers of individual human beings, the administrators and teachers and students, who collectively constitute the living reality of our schools. And as in any large, heterogeneous human population, the range and diversity of values, attitudes, behaviours and personalities encountered in this one is considerable. Unquestionably, all of these factors have considerable bearing on the outcomes of any innovations attempted. We have been a long time in recognising these basic facts and probably have not fully come to grips with them yet. But our progress in doing so may be measured by the conceptual variety and philosophical diversity of the change models we will be considering here. It therefore seems appropriate to group them according to certain basic philosophical sympathies of approach.

As the reader will quickly discover, the models in question are not necessarily highly detailed, rigidly delineated constructs representing the progression of change step by step. Nor are they, in many cases, strictly the products of a single mind or study. Rather, they represent prevailing winds or trends in change theory, in which a somewhat loose accretion of more or less harmonious ideas grows up around a core concept articulated by one or more authors. As with the process of change itself, the evolution of educational change theory entails a great deal of interaction and mutual adaptation on the part of many individuals, groups and institutions and, certainly, these models reflect that interaction. There may also be considerable variation among the models we have grouped together. Despite the caveats, however, all these models do have certain things in common: they are all based on a set of assumptions about change, they are each composed of a number of distinct components or dimensions and they all contain definite implications concerning just how change is to be accomplished.

It must also be stressed that this is only a cross-section of the literature and a modest one, at that. There are many distinguished writers whose significant contributions to our understanding of change will not be included here. These include Lewin (1936), who conceptualised the need for 'unfreezing', 'change' and 'refreezing' in the course of innovation and Rogers and Shoemaker (1971), with their classic two-volume synthesis of diffusion research. Lippitt (1973) made a major contribution to the analysis, conceptualisation and visualisation of the change process; House (1981) presented three complementary perspectives on innovation: technological, political and cultural;

and Elmore (1978) proposed four organisational models of change, which together give 'a thumbnail sketch of the implementation process'. Our concern, however, is less with the full range of specific models than with broad model groupings or types and their implications for practitioners. Accordingly, I have tried to focus on some of the best known, most influential and most widely discussed change models, grouping them under a few basic types that suggest their essential philosophical and practical differences and discussing the key characteristics of each model so grouped. The classification scheme is summarised in the accompanying chart (see Figure 2.1). I attempt to elucidate precisely what these models, singly and collectively, can tell us that is of immediate, practical value in terms of the problems and processes unfolding in our schools today and also to point out what fundamental problems or processes they may have failed to address.

Type One: Product-focused Change
The models I have chosen to group under type one vary widely in their particulars, but all of them in some sense focus on the delivery of an innovative product to schools and on getting that product adopted. Naturally, since education is so much a people-oriented endeavour, attention must also be paid to the human, inter-personal aspects of change; these models do this, too, to varying degrees. But their primary emphasis is on change as a product available in discrete, instantly recognisable containers that are waiting to be placed in schools; the personal, psychological considerations are seen chiefly as potential or actual impediments to accomplishing that end. The examples given here are arranged on the basis of specificity, starting with the most general and philosophical and gradually moving toward the more concrete and technical in outlook.

Empirical-rational Approach.
Chin and Benne (1969) identified three broad categories of models of planned change: the empirical-rational, the norm-ative-re-educative and the power-coercive. As their titles suggest, they are distinguished from each other by the underlying assumptions that each makes about human behaviour and how it can be changed. The empirical-rational approach will be considered under type one, the normative-re-educative under

Figure 2.1:   A Simple Typology of Change Models

	Product-focused	System-centred	Other
Chin & Benne's Categories			
1969			
Empirical-rational	X		
Normative-re-educative		X	
Power-coercive			X
Havelock's Categories			
1971			
Social Interaction	X		
Research, Development, Diffusion	X		
Problem Solver		X	
Organisational Development		X	
Linkage Model			X

type two and the power-coercive will be examined separately, as a 'misfit' or 'nonfit'.

The primary assumption of the empirical-rational approach is, not surprisingly, that people are rational and therefore that they can be appealed to by their fellows on a rational basis. Allied with this idea is the notion that improvement, and therefore progress, are in some sense natural outgrowths of rational behaviour. For the change facilitator, this suggests that individuals, and by extension, groups, will adopt a given change if it can be rationally justified and shown to be in their own best interests.

These ideas, of course, are firmly rooted in the Enlightenment-based liberal arts tradition that is the cornerstone of the whole educational system in most Western countries. Indeed, the very concept of universal public education is a corollary to the belief in fundamental human rationality. Scientific research, so the argument goes, will gradually advance the frontiers of knowledge and thereby the potential greatly and continually to improve the quality of human life. But since ignorance and superstition are the major impediments to the spread of reason, these must be eliminated; and at the same time, the new knowledge must be disseminated. Hence, the central importance of schools, as the principal means of achieving both these ends.

In a sense, then, empirical-rational models of change may be said to be extensions of the underlying rationale of the very thing they seek to change: the schools themselves. From this viewpoint, the process of educational change simply mirrors the inevitable natural advance of overall human progress. The primacy of basic and applied research and the general dissemination of knowledge through schools are taken as givens. All that is needed to accelerate the pace of change are strategies that will remove impediments. Thus, in these models, great emphasis is placed on improved personnel selection and replacement, to ensure that those who are responsible for improving educational practice will, in fact, do so and that those unwilling or unable to do so will be removed from key positions. Similarly, from an organisational standpoint, the use of systems analysts and other scientific management experts who can analyse a complex educational system and determine how it might be made to function more efficiently is hailed as a promising means of focusing and directing future school improvement efforts. In a parallel if somewhat more abstract vein, clarification of language as a means of increasing semantic and conceptual precision and thereby of facilitating more effective interpersonal communication as a tool for implementing change is also stressed. Finally, Utopian thinking is recognised as a viable strategy for change, since a rationally persuasive vision of a 'better' future, extrapolated from currently available knowledge, could be used to encourage the trial and adoption of innovations by practitioners.

As already indicated, the strategies associated with the empirical-rational approach are for the most part extremely vague, general formulations having little or no direct reference to concrete situations. Little clear distinction is made between individuals, who in any event are seen as rational but passive receivers of change, and larger groups, or between specific innovation products and improvement in a general sense. The implication is that innovation, whether as a new curriculum package or simply a 'better idea', will or will not be disseminated and adopted in schools in accordance with some mutual dynamic of the various components we have mentioned. Thus, in its hazy idealism and lack of detail, the empirical-rational model typifies the approach to change commonly taken by the early developers and would-be innovators and reformers of the late 50s and 60s.

Social Interaction. Like Chin and Benne, Havelock (1971, 1973) also identified three categories of change models, though from a more detailed, pragmatic viewpoint. Two of these models, social interaction and research, development and diffusion (RD&D), will be considered under our type one rubric; the third, problem solver, will be examined later.

Perhaps the most fundamental difference between the empirical-rational and social interaction models is that the former, as we have seen, emphasises the supposed rational character of human beings, whether as individuals or groups; the latter, on the other hand, plainly takes the individual as the unit of analysis. As in the first case, however, it is ultimately not possible to draw a rigid distinction between the two since, at least in the case of schools, the individual is very much part of a group as well. This is brought out clearly in the assumptions which support the social interaction models. These five basic assumptions are as follows:

1) Individuals belong to a network of social relations which influences their behaviour;

2) The rate of acceptance of innovations by individuals may be predicted based on each individual's place in the network;

3) Informal personal contact is vital to the adoption process;

4) Group membership and reference group identifications are major predictors of adoption for individuals;

5) The rate of diffusion in a social system follows a predictable S-curve pattern: initially slow, then very rapid, then returning to a long, slow period.

Social interaction models envisage a five-stage innovation process. The first stage, awareness of the innovation by a potential user, is followed by growing interest in it and active information seeking. The third stage, evaluation of the innovation based on the information gained, may lead to a trial stage and finally, if the trial is deemed successful, to adoption. These models also recognise, however, that rejection can abort the process at any point; and this recognition provides the impetus for the disseminative and facilitative behaviours that constitute a large part of the model's practical applications.

Because of its focus on the individual and its view of change as chiefly a question of inducing practitioners to adopt an innovation, this model pays a good deal of attention to effective means of encouraging a potential user to do so. These sources of influence or information vary at different innovation stages and, together, they offer added insights into the nature of the change process. The general pattern seems to be a gradual movement from the external and impersonal to an increasingly personalised and ultimately internalised process. At the awareness phase, impersonal, external sources are likely to be the most important, since in practice most educational innovations are externally mandated, arriving in the school like strangers knocking on one's classroom door. As interest increases and more information about the innovation is sought, the mass media and the weighty words of experts are still likely to be highly influential, though at this stage personal contacts may also begin to carry some weight. At the evaluation and trial stages, personal sources assume even greater importance; and finally, in addressing the question of adoption, individuals will use their own personal judgement.

Because the social interaction model views individuals according to their place within a specific social network, internal information flow is emphasised and most of the specific strategies and tactics associated with the model aim at utilising or influencing that flow. At the same time, there is a kind of calculated indirection informing most of these behaviours, since change is still ultimately viewed as a natural process and excessively active facilitation efforts might be seen as unwarranted tampering or interference. The suggestion is that, within the social network, individuals rely primarily on each other and look to their own opinion leaders, rather than somewhat suspect outsiders, as primary sources of information.

Thus, the 'quasi-strategies' identified by Havelock (1973, p. 160) include natural diffusion, which asserts that after ten to twenty percent of a given population has passed through the five stages and adopted an innovation, most of the rest will inevitably follow. Utilisation of natural communication networks is also stressed: change agents are encouraged to identify local opinion leaders and existing circles of influence and to target them in disseminating information. As an extension of this idea, network building is seen as a means of promoting informal contacts. And finally, multi-media approaches, in which different media are correlated with different stages in the adoption process in order to maximise effectiveness in reaching diverse individuals, are favoured.

The social interaction model, then, though somewhat more specific than the empirical-rational approach, still shares with it a fundamental vision of change as a natural process that, though it may be encouraged by appropriate actions, will nonetheless unfold in semi-automatic fashion despite the differing responses of individuals to it. And though facilitation is addressed in the concept of stage-appropriate influences and the several strategies it suggests, there is still a critical lack of concrete, practitioner-oriented information here concerning how to apply the model to the problems of real people in a real school.

<u>Research, Development and Diffusion</u>. Havelock's second category of change models (1971, 1973) differs primarily in terms of scope. Change is here seen as an extended, large-scale process and accordingly, detailed planning and development are emphasised. Like the empirical-rational model, RD&D stresses rationality: change is believed to proceed in an orderly, planned sequence, from research to development to packaging to dissemination. From this assumption follows the need for careful planning, which will elaborate and coordinate the necessary division of labour in keeping with the rational sequence. Naturally, this kind of expertise-intensive, highly organised approach to innovation is also very costly, particularly in the planning and development phases. But it is assumed that, in the long run, the innovation's high quality, efficient design and widespread applicability will more than justify the initial cost.

Since change itself is perceived as rational and a host of experts with their specialised skills are utilised, the whole process becomes extremely methodical, progressing in an orderly fashion from problem identification through production of an appropriate solution to its diffusion. As in the other type one models, the target of the innovation is here seen almost exclusively as a passive receiver. In its fullest form, the RD&D model includes four components which are research, development, diffusion and adoption, and which are in turn divided into subparts. But in reality, few RD&D models actually include the full range of activities and for the most part, as in the previous models, attention is focused on the early stages leading up to the adoption of the innovation package.

In brief, the theory is that research provides the raw materials from which an innovation may be developed. Development, then, consists of invention which is the initial conceptualisation of the innovation, and design in which that concept is transformed into an appropriate functional package. We then proceed to diffusion, which consists of dissemination, aimed at generating widespread awareness of the innovation, and demonstration of it for potential adopters, so that they may evaluate its utility. The final component, adoption, includes three subdivisions: trial, installation and institutionalisation. Once a 'successful' trial has been undertaken, so the theory goes, the innovation needs to be 'installed' in the institution on an operational basis. Finally, in order to ensure lasting change, the innovation must be changed into a 'non-innovation': that is, it must be so integrated into the institution that it is no longer seen as a change but as part of established procedure.

In the diffusion and adoption stages, this model seems to overlap with the social interaction model, except that there is little emphasis on the individual or on individual differences in rate of response. The assumption seems to be that expertly designed and disseminated innovation products will not produce such ambiguous problem responses. As we saw in the previous chapter, however, this is not necessarily the case. In any event, these latter stages seem to get the least specific attention in most RD&D models.

Most of the strategies commonly identified with this model, not surprisingly, are overwhelmingly technical in emphasis and are heavily weighted toward the development end of the innovation spectrum. The development of high performance, 'user-proof' products and the construction of information systems to provide channels for diffusion are stressed. The same technical approach is applied to dissemination: elaborate programmes, including planning, packaging, preparation for the target audience, multi-media presentations, follow-up and evaluation procedures, are visualised as helping to spread the innovation package. Other RD&D strategies include legislated change and its sibling, the fait accompli strategy. Both of these attempt to bypass or take for granted the earlier phases of change in the model, and go straight to installation. To balance these somewhat impatient approaches, the strategies of experimental social innovation and systems analysis are more gradual and tentative in outlook, favouring field testing and productive interaction between an ideal model and actual current practice.

To carry out these strategies, a variety of research-oriented tactics are employed, such as hypothesising, design, sampling and instrumentation. In addition, development and diffusion tactics come into play. These include: experimental demonstration, user need surveys, evaluation of adoption success or failure and successive approximation, by means of which a purely theoretical model is gradually converted into a practical, functional one.

Although these various components, strategies and tactics, taken together, appear to offer a detailed, systematic approach to change, a great

deal is still left to the imagination. The plain
fact is that all of them are still far too theoretical to be of much practical value. In this they do
not differ essentially from the other models included in our type one grouping.

Conclusions. Despite their apparent differences,
then, all of our type one models also seem to have a
lot in common. Although their theoretical language
about change may vary, in practice they all seem to
take a fairly narrow view of it, focusing on a
particular innovation package or product and the
attempt to get it adopted in an institution. To
varying degrees, all three of these models seem to
visualise change as a natural, if not inevitable,
process, though they differ in the degree of help
they try to offer nature in effecting adoption. The
assumption appears to be that, if the innovation
product is 'good', and, at least according to the
RD&D model, the development efforts of so many
experts ought to ensure that it is, it will necessarily be adopted. And though the latter two
approaches do pay at least some attention to implementation, this remains minimal and excessively
general, at best.
    Perhaps the most glaring omission in these
models is the lack of attention to the role of
change facilitator. This vital component in the
change process is either not mentioned at all or
superficially glossed over; nowhere do we find a
specific elaboration of who this person is, and what
she or he is actually supposed to do in order to
accomplish the grand, broadly stated goals each
model describes. The fact is that these models are
fundamentally descriptive rather than pragmatic in
nature, and this appears to lie at the root of a lot
of their problems. For it is certainly far easier
to describe a desired or imagined state of affairs
in general terms than it is to specify behaviours
and detailed procedures for attaining it. Paradoxically, at the same time that these models so neglect
the role of change facilitator, they also take an
overwhelmingly passive view of the institution or
individual practitioner as receivers of a preconceived, fully formed change product that is delivered to them. There is some range among the type
one models, of course, and a gradual shift toward
increased emphasis on interpersonal relations may
perhaps be discerned. The social interaction model,
at least, could be said to portray the individual in

a somewhat less passive light; but even there we find little suggestion of active involvement on the part of individuals in promoting or guiding change. Who, then, is responsible for promoting change? How, in fact, is it to happen?

In the words of Goodlad (1975), 'We need research to find out what is likely to get through. But just an idea is not sufficient. There must be a vehicle and an infrastructure to carry the idea, plant it and, subsequently, nourish it' (p. 178). Clearly, this 'vehicle' or 'infrastructure' and the nourishing function it must perform are aspects of change that we cannot afford to overlook. In our next set of models we encounter a fundamentally different approach to educational innovation, one which appears to answer at least some of the questions we have raised in connection with the type one group.

Type Two: System-centred Change

The models in type two employ a radically different concept of what change is and, therefore, how we go about achieving it. Essentially, these models attempt to make the system 'better' by 'improving' the individuals who collectively comprise it and by teaching the institution as a whole how to improve itself. Improvement in this sense is something much broader and, perhaps, harder to define than the mechanistic, product-delivery conception of educational innovation in the type one models. Accordingly, the whole conceptual framework within which the type two models operate represents a radical shift in emphasis. Instead of the logical, rationalistic arguments supporting the first group, these models are based on the tenets of humanistic psychology, which stress nonhierarchical, personal interactions and maximum communication. And because of their more general nature, the type two models are even closer to one another than those in the first group were. To a great extent, in fact, they are merely alternative formulations of a common concept.

Normative-re-educative Approach.

This second of the three change model groupings elaborated by Chin and Benne (1969) takes immediate exception to the assumptions of the type one models in its view of individuals as being actively in search of ways to satisfy their needs and interests. Far from passively receiving the prepackaged, fully formed innovations delivered to them, they are seen to be active participants in all phases of the change process. Further, since the individual is also a member of society, the society's norms and institutions will play a significant part in guiding the nature of the individual's participation. And this recognition of the importance of social values and practices, as opposed to the purely rational consideration addressed by the empirical-rational model, has its counterpart on the personal level in the belief that values, habits and other normative structures and roles, as well as rational responses to new information, are vital to the change process. Thus, in the normative-re-educative approach, strict rationality is not enough, because human motivation, in practice, is not a strictly rational question. What is needed, according to this model, is a total re-education or normative restructuring for each individual; and this cannot be imposed from without. Rather, if the change is to have any substance and duration, individuals must take an active part in their own re-education.

Perhaps the most fundamental aspect of the normative-re-educative approach is the open, collaborative and highly flexible relationship between client and change agent. Far from being seen as a technical expert who can deliver a ready-made solution to the client, the change agent is a mediator, a facilitator and communicator who works with the client first to identify and then to solve the client's problems. There is, in fact, no prior assumption that technical information alone can resolve them; rather, the belief is that problems more likely lie in the attitudes, values or norms of the various relationships within the client system. Thus, the change agent's task in this model would include the uncovering and public examination of previously unrecognised impediments, presumably leading to their resolution. This would be accomplished using methods and concepts taken from the behavioural sciences, in keeping with the model's central focus on clarification and reconstruction of values.

There are two basic approaches to change that are commonly found in normative-re-educative models. The first focuses on improving the problem-solving capabilities of the system; thus, change is considered a collective, systematic, institutional form of problem solving. In applying this approach, the individuals within the system actively participate in problem identification and resolution. The change agent's interventions would vary at different stages, but could include: data collection, provision of feedback and collaborative planning; training of managers and others in problem solving through self-examination; developing acceptance of feedback; and training internal change agents to carry out research, consultation and training: in short, to fulfil the external change agent's role themselves, thus enabling the client system to become self-sufficient in change.

The second approach takes the individual as the unit of change. From this perspective, constructive change is visualised as primarily a question of removing obstructions and thereby enabling the assumed positive directions of human potential to be fully realised. Thus, the change agent's interventions concentrate on fostering personal growth in individuals. This is done by means of personal counselling, training groups, and other controlled group interactions such as workshops, labs and T-groups designed to permit personal confrontations in a supportive, trusting atmosphere and to utilise both verbal and nonverbal means of communication to induce continuing growth.

In both these approaches, the specific labs and workshops used, as well as the change agent's very presence in the school, are seen as temporary interventions intended to promote long-term, lasting change. The assumption is that once the client system has learned to examine, diagnose and treat itself, or correspondingly, once the process of personal growth and expansion has been successfully launched in individuals within the system, a positive, ongoing process of growth and improvement will follow. The experience-based learning promoted by the normative-re-educative models and the open communication, enhanced trust and lowering of barriers they try to foster will, it is believed, accomplish a fundamental re-education of the participants which will, in turn, lead to change in a more formal sense.

Problem Solver. Another very similar formulation is Havelock's third change model category, the problem solver approach (1971, 1973). Like the normative-re-educative, the problem solver model is firmly grounded in the group dynamics, human relations tradition. Once again, user need is considered the primary concern, and the client is to be actively involved in identifying those needs. Consequently, this model also presents the change agent as a 'nonexpert' whose relationship with the client is collaborative, not directive. Additionally, internal resources and self-initiated and -applied innovation as a basis for strong user commitment are emphasised.

The problem solver model views change as embracing seven stages. The first stage manifests the client's awareness of the need for change and desire for external assistance. In the second stage, client system and change agent work together to establish a harmonious change relationship. Having accomplished this, the next stage is collaboratively to diagnose the client's problems. Stage four addresses the problems that have been identified and formulates plans for resolving them. In stage five, the planned innovation is actually adopted; stage six is concerned with stabilising or institutionalising the change. The final stage is termination of the client system/change agent relationship once the change has been stabilised and the client has developed the requisite problem-solving skills. This analogue to the patient/therapist relationship recognises that, at a certain point, dependency on an external agent for problem resolution becomes counterproductive.

Numerous strategies have been derived from the problem solver model; these include system self-renewal, action research, collaborative action inquiry, the human relations laboratory and consultation. Once again, they all stress maximum collaborative interaction and communication, and the fostering of internal problem solving capacity. Some common tactics relevant to the problem solver approach would include the use of T-groups, sensitivity training groups, reflection, authentic feedback, role playing, group observation and process analysis, survey feedback, brainstorming and synectics.

Certainly, it would be possible to explore the problem solver model in greater detail than we have so far. But for our present purposes, this may not be necessary. At any rate, perhaps the best way to convey to the reader the essence of the problem solver approach is to consider its best known representative, Organisational Development (OD).

Organisational Development. One of the best known strategies for change, and one that typifies the problem solver approach, is organisational development. Interestingly, OD was originally intended for use in business organisations and was subsequently adapted to the needs of schools. It should also be noted that OD was conceived as a practical strategy for change, not a model or theory. But, at least within the somewhat broad context of this chapter, it serves much the same function as the other models and we will consider it as such.

As its name suggests, organisational development focuses on the group and its dynamics; individuals are considered primarily as functional units within the system. According to this model, schools are systems of people working interdependently at a variety of tasks and collaborating with different subgroups as they move from one task to another. A tri-level perspective is used to characterise these interactions, distinguishing between what happens at the interpersonal level, the subsystem level and the level of the organisation as a whole. To the extent that these various levels of interactions can be made to function more effectively, it is believed, many change-related problems will be resolved and the quality of those solutions will also be higher.

One of the major goals of OD is to foster more effective functioning of what are called subsystems. These are conceptual entities consisting of people, supplies, space and information which carry out the various tasks that together constitute the school. The ultimate objective of organisational development is to promote greater organisational adaptability; to accomplish this, improvement in both interpersonal skills and subsystem effectiveness are stressed. Schmuck et al. (1977) describe seven interdependent capabilities, operant on both the interpersonal and subsystem levels, that are necessary for subsystem effectiveness. These are: clarifying communication, establishing goals, uncovering and working with conflict, improving group meeting procedures, problem solving, decision making and assessing changes. Development of all of these skills tends to reduce conflict, boost productivity and generally to help remove obstructions to efficient functioning both within and between subsystems.

Practical experience has shown that successful implementation of OD is dependent on a number of variables (Schmuck et al., 1977). Foremost among these is the organisation's genuine readiness to undertake it. Strong management support, both by headteachers and LEA personnel, is essential; they must also be prepared to acknowledge openly and publicly that the existing state of affairs in the school is less than ideal. In general, open and effective communication among school personnel is crucial if true collaborative efforts and sufficient common agreement on educational goals are to be achieved. And in order to maximise the likelihood of successful implementation, leadership continuity is important.

Perhaps the most vital aspect of successful organisational development, though, is time. In the early stages, there must be sufficient time to introduce OD and its working methods to the organisation; subsequently, an equivalent amount of quality time is required to accomplish the major goals. Within a single academic year, it is estimated that approximately 160 hours of direct OD work by each staff member would be required in a moderately large school, assuming that it had already reached an appropriate level of readiness.

As with our other type two change models, OD requires the active participation of trained and skilled consultants, especially during the introduction and implementation phases. Typically, these consultants use four main types of interventions: training, data feedback, confrontation and process observation and feedback (Schmuck et al., 1977). In the case of large-scale change efforts, additional interventions such as problem solving, planning, establishing a continuing OD task force and modifying technostructural activities of the client system may also be employed (Schmuck & Miles, 1971). In any event, the development and increasing use of internal consultants is vitally important. Failure to do so can threaten the achievement of institutionalisation, which is said to have been realised when funding for OD is included in the school or LEA budget, when it is carried out by internal staff members who continue to train others in the requisite skills and when it is perceived to be the accepted operational norm for the organisation.

Limitations of Type Two Models. As stated at the outset, the type two models work on broad organisational and individual goals, rather than focusing on specific changes. This can contribute to difficulties in assessment, since the stated objectives of the models may not be readily quantifiable or measurable. Even on a less formal basis, evaluation would necessarily seem to rely primarily on participants' perceptions that change had, in fact, been effected.

In practical terms, however, time limitations may constitute an even more fundamental problem. Due to the inherent vagueness of the nonobjective parameters employed, it is almost a given that considerable time would be required to achieve the models' stated goals. As we saw in the case of OD, an estimated 160 hours of staff time might be needed during a single school year. This works out to approaching one hour per day for the whole staff over an entire year which, as any principal or headteacher knows, represents a massive if not patently impossible commitment on the part of what is an already overburdened staff. Indeed, given sufficient time devoted exclusively to its working out, it might be said that almost any approach to change would have a reasonable chance of accomplishing something; the problem, always, is where is this time to come from? It is perhaps significant that Fullan, Miles and Taylor (1981), despite their overall endorsement of OD as 'a useful strategy for school improvement' (p. 58), concluded that '...the probability that any given OD programme, in or out of schools, will be "successful" is perhaps 0.5 or less. Failures are as likely as success' (pp.49-50). The authors immediately qualify those less-than-optimistic findings based on problems in the research methodologies and data collection, asserting that OD, although a complex and labour-intensive strategy, can be effective if correctly used. But from a practical standpoint, it is questionable whether such a time-consuming, labour-intensive approach is really feasible in schools as they exist today.

The real problem, then, seems to be that OD in particular, and the problem solver and normative-reeducative models in general, tend to ignore the practical realities of our schools. Institutions peopled by overburdened, underpaid staff and plagued by lack of time and dwindling resources in the face of escalating demands for better performance, higher standards and more attention to special needs hardly seem to represent the kind of ideal, receptive, energetic and creative clients visualised by these models. In addition, both the skills and relationships the models emphasise are, for the most part, quite foreign to the prevalent school climate in most countries. The degree of openness and free communication, not to mention ambiguity, that must be tolerated during the lengthy adoption and implementation period might not be sustainable or

acceptable to many schools. At any rate, realistically speaking, it would appear that these issues
and questions require a good deal more attention
than the type two models have given them.

Type Three and Beyond...

As noted earlier, I have attempted to simplify our
survey of change models by grouping the various
examples into two basic types on a broad conceptual
basis. It is to be hoped that some clarity has been
gained in the process. Unfortunately, though,
reality is rarely simple, not even the limited
reality of theoretical models. Accordingly, there
are some remaining models, even in this modest list,
that don't fit neatly into either of our major
types. The last two change models we will be
examining here, the power-coercive and linkage
models, will be considered in relation to our two
major type groupings.

Power-coercive Approach.

The last of Chin and
Benne's (1969) three models addresses a somewhat
different facet of institutional change. Extremely
broad in scope, this approach attempts to foment
change through the promulgation of new laws or
policies: a kind of change by decree. As its name
suggests, power is more overtly employed in this
approach than in any of the others. Of course,
power or influence in some sense is necessarily a
part of all human group interactions; but it is not
always conceived or utilised in quite the same way.
In the empirical-rational approach, knowledge is the
primary source of power; normative-re-educative
models, while recognising the power of knowledge,
expand their focus to include 'noncognitive determi-
nants of behaviour' (p. 52) such as values, attitudes and feelings. The power-coercive approach, on
the other hand, primarily emphasises political and
economic power and their potential to impact the
greater social system.
    There are several major strategies associated
with this model. One that has been widely employed
in promoting social change is nonviolence. Peaceful
demonstrations, sit-ins and economic boycotts, as
well as forceful and eloquent public speaking, are
all nonviolent means of manipulating the power
structure. In addition to their political and
economic components, many nonviolent strategies also

effectively utilise moral power as a catalyst for public opinion and political action.

The use of political institutions to effect change is another power-coercive strategy. As we saw in Chapter One, many widespread, sweeping changes have been mandated by legislation at the national or regional level during the last few decades. This strategy continues to be widely employed today. Besides legislation, judicial decisions, such as those mandating school desegregation and student bussing in the United States, may also significantly impact policy. A sister strategy to this is effecting change through the recomposition and manipulation of existing power elites. This could be accomplished by persuading legislators and other decisionmakers to support a desired change, or by working for the election of different public officeholders, and thereby changing the composition and behaviour of the relevant decisionmaking bodies.

The power-coercive model is similar to the empirical-rational approach in its broad scope and rational emphasis. The main difference is that, instead of relying solely on the power of rational argument to convince, this model also employs other tactics in its efforts to affect the existing power structure. In practice, however, there appear to be severe limits to the effectiveness of this approach. Even the most successful legislative campaign or the most far-reaching judicial decision may result in little, if any, change in actual practice. In addition, certain types of change lend themselves much more readily than others to political or economic manipulation; the classroom practices of teachers, for example, which must be of so much concern to anyone interested in educational change, do not appear to be easily or meaningfully affected by broad political mandates. Because of these limitations, then, the power-coercive model would have to be combined with another approach in order to accomplish real and lasting change. This could be either a type one or a type two model, or some sort of hybrid like our final example, the linkage model.

Linkage Model. The linkage model is more a category of change theory and practice than a specific set of elaborations by a particular person; as such, there is no one source to which we can refer for descriptive information. Rather, various researchers have contributed to the conceptualisation of this approach.

The basic concept of linkage is the establishment of communication networks and interaction between sources of innovative products or practices and practitioners who might use them, by means of an intermediary facilitator. This could be either a linking agent or a linking agency. Paul (1977) identifies five components of typical models: user problem solving, need sensing, client-centred solution building, solution-processing channels and micro-system building. The reader will recognise many of these concerns from our descriptions of the type two models. But other linkage model characteristics identified by Hood (1982), such as helping to disseminate new products or practices resulting from systematic research and development and providing feedback from educators to the information resource specialists, are strongly reminiscent of RD&D, a type one model.

What most distinguishes this approach is its focus on the linking agent or agency, whether internal or external. Internal linkers are persons or groups within the school or LEA who are concerned with system improvement. External linkers may be found in education agencies, departments or research units in colleges or universities, educational networks or organisations serving multiple-component systems. Nash and Culbertson (1977) cite three distinguishing characteristics of linking agents: 'First, linking agents direct their actions at the improvement of individual or institutional performance. Second, they use knowledge or knowledge-based products and services as key instruments of improvement. Thirdly, in order to connect those engaged in change with ideas, findings, descriptions of practices, training materials and other needed knowledge-based products, they must perform boundary-spanning roles' (pp. 2-3). Here again, the hybrid nature of this model is readily apparent. The first of these factors falls clearly under our type two, the second under type one and the third, which perhaps best embodies the essence of the linkage concept, is analogous to elements found in models under both of these type groupings.

The key function of the linking agent, whether internal or external, is to bridge the gap between theoreticians and practitioners, who are perceived to inhabit different and often incompatible systems. By this means a two-way information flow is stimulated, leading to an increase in acquisition and use of relevant ideas, products and services by practitioners, a greater relevance and timeliness in the projects being developed by researchers and generally closer and more meaningful collaboration between the two groups. Many writers have described a broad but overlapping array of roles, functions and skills for linkers. Despite this abundant attention, however, it remains somewhat difficult to draw a composite picture of the successful linking agent. Crandall (1977) characterises the 'complete linking agent' as a generalist who has acquired a broad array of skills and understandings, and who specialises in resource utilisation and effective interaction with clients. Thus, both formidable human relations abilities and an ample command of a wide range of technical skills would seem to be required.

One example of the linkage model in action was the R&D Utilization (RDU) Program, funded by the National Institute of Education, which was designed to deliver innovative services and resources to client schools. A study of seven demonstration projects attempted to evaluate the effectiveness of the kind of interorganisational networks favoured by the linking strategy. In 'an overwhelming majority of the schools' examined, an externally developed innovation had been adopted and implemented. School personnel were pleased, continued use was planned and, overall, the projects were considered to be highly successful (Louis & Rosenblum, 1981). Three general characteristics of successful linking models identified by the study were: degree of field agent initiative in providing services, amount of field agent time on site and total amount of training given school personnel.

As we have seen, the linkage model includes various characteristics shared by some of our type one and type two models. In its emphasis on an intermediary or middle role, however, it inevitably places limits on its own scope, focusing mainly on dissemination and introduction of information, products and techniques. In order successfully to carry out the avowed boundary-spanning role and to see the innovation through to institutionalisation, other approaches, whether normative-re-educative or empirical-rational, would still need to be employed. Thus linkage, like power-coercive, at best offers only a partial perspective on change.

ALL ROADS LEAD TO--WHERE?

Having completed our brief sampling of a number of prominent conceptual models of change, we may reasonably pause to inquire what exactly we have learned from them and where it has taken us. Certainly, we have encountered a considerable range of approaches to change in education, all of which could be said to have contributed useful perspectives or ideas. But, without exception, the models we have examined suffer from one or more glaring deficiencies, which severely limit their utility for practitioners.

To begin with, almost all of these models are far too theoretical in outlook. The theories, as we have seen, may vary considerably, but the net effect of this over reliance on preconceived ideas about both educational institutions and change itself is problematic in all cases. Some of them, such as the empirical-rational models, suffer from excessive vagueness, which makes any practical application difficult in the extreme, since as soon as we attempt to move from broad, descriptive generalities to more concrete bases for action, the real meaning and intent of these models become highly ambiguous, at best. Other type one models, though admittedly more detailed, are still more concerned with their respective theoretical formulations than with what may actually be happening in schools. And the type two models, though perhaps less overtly theoretical in one sense, nonetheless seem over dependent on an extremely idealistic view of schools. This may account, at least in part, for the high reported failure rate cited for the OD approach.

Another problem common to almost all the models is their narrow focus. This is particularly ironic in view of their emphatically theoretical nature, which might be expected to encourage wide-ranging flights of fancy. The type one models, as we have seen, focus primarily on adoption, to the detriment of later phases. The type two and, to some extent, the linkage models, may venture somewhat farther down the road, but despite their idealism, they remain for the most part surprisingly limited in scope and at the same time far removed from the realities of most schools. In this, they seem not to have gained much in either direction. And in any case, the type two models are less likely to be looking at a particular, concrete innovation, that could be unambiguously identified and whose course could be plotted with some objectivity. The plain fact is that none of these models really encompasses the full range of the change process, although some (such as RD&D) do at least pay lip service to it.

Hand in hand with the problems of excessive vagueness and/or theoretical orientation is a lack of concern for the vital practical role of change facilitator. In the type one models, in fact, the CF is scarcely even mentioned. The type two and linkage models, though they certainly recognise the existence and importance of the CF, remain woefully short on specifics. There is no lack of descriptions of the change agent's needed skills and possible behaviours, but, particularly in the case of internal change agents, exactly who these people are and how they are to acquire the skills and carry out the tasks described by the various models are questions not adequately addressed. As the linkage model itself states, the gap between theoretician and practitioner is considerable; nowhere is this more apparent than in the discrepancy between their respective views of who the people are who will receive and carry out the innovations meant to change and to improve our schools.

Finally and perhaps most importantly of all, none of these models truly grapples with the knotty question of evaluation. Scant attention is paid by any of them to assessing the success or failure of a change effort and none at all to how to evaluate the state of affairs <u>during the process of change</u>. Headteachers, change agents and others involved in initiating and implementing an innovation need to know what is going on in order to be able to respond appropriately and thus, to help ensure that the process continues to evolve. Given the nature of change in schools, short-term, snap judgements of the 'success' or 'failure' of an innovation are worse than meaningless; at the same time, waiting around for the results of long-term, in-depth assessments is of little immediate use to practitioners, for by that time, whatever problems may have arisen will have gone beyond the point where effective steps could be taken to resolve or to defuse them. What, then, are principals, CFs, and other prospective managers of change to do?

Meaningful evaluation of the fluid, current status of an ongoing change effort requires a subtler, more indepth understanding of the subprocesses of change, and the range of behaviours that may be associated with each, than we have found in any of the models we have examined here. Rather than theoretical formulations based on one or another philosophical premise about the nature of human beings, or broadly idealistic approaches to human 'improvement' in which concrete innovations and results may get lost or forgotten altogether, what practitioners may find most useful is a detailed understanding of change that will be immediately and concretely applicable to any innovation proposed in any school. In Chapter Three, then, we explore the various subprocesses of change from a practitioner's viewpoint, in order to provide this essential underpinning to the successful prosecution of an innovation effort.

REFERENCES

Chin, R. & Benne, K.D. (1969). General strategies for effecting changes in human systems. In W.G. Bennis, K.D. Benne, & R. Chin (Eds.) The planning of change (2nd edition). New York: Holt, Rinehart & Winston, Inc.

Crandall, D. P. (1977). Training and supporting linking agents. In N. Nash & J. Culbertson (Eds.) Linking processes in educational improvement, concepts and applications. Columbus, Ohio: University Council for Educational Administration.

Elmore, R. E. (1978). Organizational models of social program implementation. In D. Mann (Ed.) Making change happen? New York: Teachers College Press, Columbia University.

Fullan, M., Miles, M.B., & Taylor, G. (1981, February). Organizational development in schools: The state of the art. Washington, D.C.: National Institute of Education.

Goodlad, J.I. (1975). The dynamics of educational change: Toward responsive schools. New York: McGraw-Hill.

Havelock, R. G. (1971). Planning for innovation through dissemination and utilization of knowledge. Ann Arbor, MI: Institute for Social Research, University of Michigan.

Havelock, R.G. (1973). The change agent's guide to innovation in education. Englewood Cliffs, NJ: Educational Technology Publications.

Hood, P.D. (1982). The role of linking agents in school improvement: A review, analysis, and synthesis of recent major studies. San Francisco, Far West Laboratory for Educational Research and Development.

House, E.R. (1981). Three perspectives of innovations: Technological, political, and cultural. In R. Lehming & M. Kane (Eds.) Improving schools: Using what we know. Beverly Hills, CA: Sage Publications, Inc.

Lewin, K. (1936). Principles of topological psychology. New York: McGraw-Hill Book Company.

Lippitt, G.L. (1973). Visualizing change. Fairfax, Virginia: NTL Learning Resources Corp., Inc.

Louis, K.S. & Rosenblum, S. (1981, July). Designing and managing interorganizational networks. Washington, D.C.: U.S. Department of Education/National Institute of Education.

Mort, P.R. (1953). Educational adaptability. The School Executive, 71, 1-23.

Nash, N. & Culbertson, J. (1977). Introduction. In N. Nash & J. Culbertson (Eds.) Linking processes in educational improvement, concepts and applications. Columbus, Ohio: University Council for Educational Administration.

Paul, D.A. (1977). Change processes at the elementary, secondary, and post-secondary levels of education. In N. Nash & J. Culbertson (Eds.) Linking processes in educational improvement, concepts and applications. Columbus, Ohio: University Council for Educational Administration.

Rogers, E.M., & Shoemaker, F.F. (1971). Communication of innovations: A cross cultural approach (2nd edition). New York: Free Press.

Schmuck, R.A., & Miles, M.B. (1971). Organizational development in schools. La Jolla, CA: University Associates.

Schmuck, R.A., Runkel, P.J., Arends, J.H., & Arends, R.A. (1977). The second handbook of organizational development in schools. Eugene, OR: Center for Educational Policy and Management.

Stake, R.E., & Easley, J.A., Jr. (1978). Case studies in science education. Washington, D.C.: U.S. Government Printing Office.

Chapter 3

THE WELL-INTENTIONED TYRANNY OF MODELS

In the preceding chapters we have explored educational innovation from various perspectives: historical, philosophical, and theoretical. In the course of this conceptual journey, we have encountered widely differing viewpoints concerning the nature of change, its probable or possible course, and how it might best be approached by those concerned with its successful realisation. As we saw in our survey of theoretical approaches to change in Chapter Two, none of the models we examined truly embraced the full scope of the change process, and all of them revealed major practical flaws or gaps. For the practitioner, at any rate, change is neither abstract, nor theoretical, nor ideal; it is, rather, a cluster of concrete problems and situations occurring within the school or LEA, and usually requiring immediate attention. Thus, change is something far more specific in its meaning for practitioners than many models imply. It is also, for the most part, a far less ideal and more pragmatic undertaking than is usually represented.

Despite these caveats, however, it should not be inferred that I am categorically opposed to all conceptual models, in principle. As we saw in Chapter One, lack of knowledge about the process of change in schools has caused the untimely demise of many potentially beneficial and workable innovations. Ignorance may indeed be bliss, but only for the blithely irresponsible, who can perhaps afford it. For the rest of us, practical knowledge is essential to the successful management of our daily affairs, and certainly, for practitioners, this includes a firm understanding of the various subprocesses of change and their mutual interactions.

In this chapter, therefore, we will examine the change process from a hands-on, practitioner-oriented perspective, trying to avoid the conceptual gaps and theoretical excesses of our Chapter Two models without losing sight of the very real and important contributions each has made to our understanding of educational change. And, for those pragmatic readers whose response to the last chapter was, 'Yes, but what does all this theory mean for me', the following extension and synthesis will, I hope, provide a valid answer.

PICTURES AND PUZZLES OF REALITY

Having thus established our position, I now somewhat paradoxically propose to offer the reader yet another change model. In its simplest form, this model might be diagrammed like this:

Assessment ==> New ==> Selection ==> Implemen-
of Current   Vision   or Devel-   tation
Situation   opment &
                         Adoption

According to this formulation, then, change begins with a rational assessment and proceeds in orderly fashion through the subsequent phases or stages until implementation is reached, just as our type one models in the previous chapter confidently predicted would happen. Those alert readers who have stayed with us through the previous chapters, however, will immediately exclaim, 'Oversimplification! Distortion! Change is not a simple linear progression, nor does it consist of such a limited number of discrete, sequential pieces! Where is Initiation? Where is Institutionalisation? No, this won't do at all!'
And, indeed, they will be right. Accordingly, let us redraw the model, in order to more accurately reflect the realities of change in schools (see Figure 3.1).
In this new model, the reader will immediately note that missing pieces have been added, and all of them have been regrouped to form a circle: the change process, which ultimately has no beginning and no end. Within this process, the respective stages have been redrawn using twin sets of arrows, to indicate their interactive, fluid nature. They are, in fact, not discrete phases or stages, but subprocesses following the same dynamic as the

Figure 3.1: A Circular Model of Change

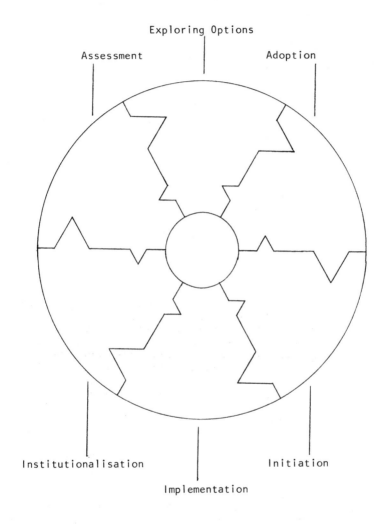

greater process of which they are part. These subprocesses are represented as identical in size and shape, to emphasise their interchangeability within the total puzzle of the change process; remove any one of them, however, and the circle breaks, the wheel no longer rolls. The smaller, central circle in the diagram represents the school, the focal point for educational innovation. Within it, each subprocess touches all the others; beyond its borders, all of them extend into the larger social context that encompasses and helps shape the school.

Before we succumb to fits of self-congratulation for having constructed such an ingenious and aesthetically pleasing picture of change, however, there are perhaps a few more questions we may want to ask ourselves. At what point does adoption end and initiation begin: when the formal, institutional decision to adopt is made? or when the innovation has been introduced into the school, and teachers are actually grappling with it? Initiation of an innovation certainly presupposes its prior adoption on some level, as well as something more--mobilisation, for example, to cite another term that writers about change sometimes use (Vandenberghe, 1982). Accordingly, we might decide to further modify our drawing in order to clarify this distinction (see Figure 3.2).

Now we've really got it, right? This time we've conceived the perfect diagram. But wait a minute. Doesn't this over emphasise initiation at the expense of later phases? Isn't this precisely the problem we so frequently encountered in our historical overview of change in Chapter One? Without implementation, surely, there is little hope for the achievement of lasting change. This being so, would it not perhaps be more accurate to view initiation as a subprocess of implementation? On this basis, we may redraw our model yet again (see Figure 3.3).

Proceeding in this manner, however, it soon becomes apparent that before long we will have no subprocesses left, but only one megaprocess. And in a sense, this might prove to be the best representation of the whole change process that we can hope to make. For the truth is that all of these are ultimately artificial distinctions, rework them how we may. The various subprocesses are merely useful conventions adopted by researchers and others to stress the complexity and evolutionary nature of change, and to enable them to talk about it from different points of view.

Figure 3.2: Initiation: Adoption and Mobilisation

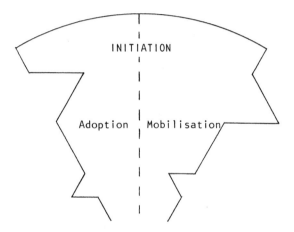

Figure 3.3:   The Relationship of Initiation and Implementation

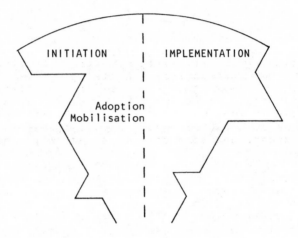

But labels, once created, have an unfortunate tendency to assume a concrete identity, often to the detriment of their original purpose. The change literature, certainly, is rife with alternative terminologies and models, and every addition to the lexicon ensures its own perpetuation, as other writers in their turn discuss and analyse it, with perhaps some further subdivisions added in the interests of clarity. It is not the intention, though, to contribute to this semantic proliferation.

Rather, what should be emphasised is that none of these theoretical, conceptual, semantic constructs has any objective reality apart from the context it seeks to elucidate. It is ideas and actions, new understandings about change and the human interactions it encompasses and triggers, that are most important, and, if our tidy, formulated charts and categories do nothing to enhance our grasp of these things, then we are better off without them. Some of the terms we employ in our discussion of subprocesses may differ from those used by other writers, as in the saying, 'Some call it a spear, and some call it an arrow'. The reader should therefore feel free to substitute whatever other terms seem most appropriate, always keeping in mind that it is not the label but the thing named that we are most concerned with. Similarly, the interlocking, circular diagram of change that we have somewhat playfully presented here is also to be taken not as any concrete, absolute, or final statement, but merely as a potentially useful tool for grasping something about the nature of this essential yet elusive process. Just as a jazz musician can construct many melodies from the same set of chord changes, one could conceive endless variations on the basic structure we have drawn. And doubtless, all of them could contribute something useful to our understanding of educational change. But our goal is to communicate concrete knowledge that is broadly and readily applicable at the operational level; therefore, as we now begin to examine in greater detail specific issues and understandings, we will restrict our attention to our original diagram, our primary melody, trying always, however, to keep an ear open to the echoes of alternative conceptions.

QUESTIONS, ANSWERS AND ESSENTIAL QUALITIES
OF CHANGE IN SCHOOLS

Perhaps more than anything else, it is the dizzying multiplicity of viewpoints with regard to change that produces the corresponding diversity of models, analyses, and other theoretical formulations that we have been concerned with. This is probably inevitable, given the complexity of our subject. So many people have a stake in schools and in attempts to change them; their functions, roles and relations to one another differ widely, and have considerable bearing on their respective views of change. This being so, one fundamental question we might ask ourselves when confronting a specific innovation or particular model would be: what is the unit of change here? and what bearing does it have on what we're seeing? Is it the single teacher in the classroom, who necessarily takes the most immediate, pragmatic approach? Is it, rather, a school-wide change that we're concerned with? Or, perhaps, an entire LEA?

In practice, of course, change may operate on any of these levels, or even all of them at once. Change often begins with a review or assessment phase, followed by an exploration of available solutions appropriate to the identified needs, and certainly this is one viable possibility. But as Rutherford and Murphy have reported (1985), it is at least equally likely that the change will arrive in the school unannounced, so to speak, having been mandated at higher administrative levels, and then seek its own de facto justification. In this sequence, adoption would precede, if not preclude, the review phase. Those readers with a strong sense of causality might find this temporal illogicality somewhat troubling; but they would, perhaps, do well to consider physicist Richard Feynman's suggestion that a positron moving forward in time is merely an electron moving backward. At any rate, for both physicist and educator, reality does not always meet our cherished expectations.

The question of top-down versus bottom-up change is one that has been given a great deal of attention without necessarily resolving anything. Some researchers (Fullan, 1982) have questioned whether top-down or mandated change can really result in meaningful school improvement and, particularly in UK, the strong tradition of teacher autonomy within the classroom has testified against it as well. Bottom-up or grass roots change does have an undeniable populist appeal, stemming as it does from the user's self-perceived needs and condition of readiness to change, and thereby obviating the onerous necessity of pressuring the potential user to accept it. But the price of spontaneity may be an inordinate amount of time spent waiting for it to occur, and the social, economic and political realities of schools today, with their growing demands for more and faster change, have increasingly promoted top-down change as an efficient and organisationally acceptable response. The fact is that either approach can be effective, if it is accompanied by the appropriate interventions, and neither one can guarantee effectiveness in and of itself.

Here again we confront the question of units and levels of change, since individual classroom teachers may well feel quite differently about top-down change from, say, a headteacher, LEA officer, or HMI. We can only repeat the previous assertion that the improvement process may be usefully applied at many different levels, simultaneously or separately. Single teachers may look around in their classrooms, discern something 'wrong', and discover a way to redress it. Headteachers may organise a school-based review, uncover problem areas, and seek appropriate means of improvement. Then again, an LEA may encounter a promising innovation fresh off the R&D presses, so to speak, and enthusiastically embrace its adoption in their schools. All these patterns are part and parcel of the process of educational change, and regardless of what level is involved, certain basic characteristics will still apply.

As our understanding of the improvement process has grown, we have learned not only to recognise these characteristics, but also to comprehend their implications, and further to express those implications in the form of comprehensive statements about educational change, its nature, and the limits it thus imposes on the form and substance, not to mention the timetable, employed with respect to a given innovation. These understandings include things that many practitioners may already know on a 'gut level', simply as part of their working 'savvy' for how to handle day-to-day affairs in the school. Indeed, they may never have consciously thought about them, at least not apart from a particular problem or question; but that is precisely the point. For both theoreticians and practitioners need to be more consciously aware of these perspectives and their implications for school improvement, in order to derive the most benefit from their application.

One of the most vital understandings about educational innovation is that, indeed, the school is a total system and every part is connected to every other, in complex, multiple, not always apparent ways. Like a balloon, if you punch on it here, it well may pop out there, almost assuredly where you would least expect it to. These unexpected consequences of change, whose appearance at least may be confidently predicted, if not their precise form, often constitute a significant impediment to successful implementation, particularly if they are not recognised as such. If, for example, an innovation requires additional time for inservice training, classroom monitoring, or individual staff conferences, ancillary changes such as retimetabling, acquiring training materials, and obtaining funds to pay supply teachers may become necessary. Furthermore, because of increased management demands on headteachers, the basic requirements for effective leadership may be significantly altered. Failure to recognise and respond to these needs could delay or even permanently stall implementation. At the same time, excessive concern with these subsidiary issues can distract vital energy from the original innovation, with perhaps no less harmful effects. This is one small illustration of the kind of constant high-wire act the head must undertake to keep these things in balance. In schooling as in ecology, the total integrity of the system must be respected above all else. This need not mean automatic perpetuation of the status quo, but neither does it imply a blind embrace of change for change's sake, without carefully considering its probable effects.

From this essential vision of the school as total system, with its accompanying concept of maintenance of vital balance as the headteacher's primary goal, come several other important considerations. The first is that, at least in most cases, major change cannot successfully be accomplished in one broad stroke. The incredible complexity of the change process, and the almost unlimited succession of 'ripples' that a given change may produce, ensure that it will take a great deal of time. More than even the admittedly formidable organisational and logistical problems an innovation may create, it is the people problems that usually present the most resistant obstacles to change (Fullan and Park, 1981). Traditions and attitudes have deep roots, and how fast they can be modified necessarily depends on the readiness, the experience and the understanding of the people involved. For the headteacher or other change facilitator, ascertaining the degree of readiness to change within the given situation must be an almost continuous activity. <u>If change is a process, so too must its management be</u>. This constant monitoring, both formal and informal, of the school situation, is another example of something doubtless familiar to many school leaders who may do it as a matter of course within their normal working day. But they may not be consciously aware, even so, of how important it can be in providing useful clues to the speed at which progress with an innovation can be made. Balance, in this sense, would therefore imply an awareness of the subtle shifts in individual attitudes that enable implementation to proceed, and the varying paces at which they happen.

Another, perhaps even subtler, aspect of balance involves the variegated web of expectations that any innovation inevitably arouses in its users. These expectations tend usually toward the extremes, which are inimical to balance in any context. As we have seen, the negative responses of teachers who anticipate more work, added stress and the inevitable discomfort that comes from grappling with the unfamiliar, can drastically affect the pace and, indeed, the final outcome of change. But even the most positive assumptions about a prospective innovation may carry dangerous implications. It seems reasonable enough to suppose that those responsible for deciding to adopt an innovation do so, at least in most cases, in expectation of achieving some tangible benefit to the school or schools in question. But those very expectations, however supportive of change, can be the source of a great many additional problems. The fact is that no single innovation, regardless of how promising it seems, can be expected to remedy all of the problems of schooling. Initially, it may well create more problems than it solves, and even in the long run no change or group of changes will eliminate the need for future innovations. And the problems, far from being isolated interruptions or violations of some trouble-free, static norm, are merely localised zones of interaction between conflicting attitudes, behaviours or other aspects of the process. A life without problems, as any practitioner well knows, is as inconceivable as an atmosphere devoid of storms.

Improvement, therefore, must also be viewed as a continual process, not as something to be 'done' within a finite sphere and then forgotten. Innovations are not panaceas and effective change facilitators must approach them with a functional blend of enthusiasm, commitment and healthy scepticism. Even while encouraging others to accept change, they must take care not to arouse in them unrealistic expectations that will soon give way to disappointment and rejection. Emotional balance is thus every bit as essential as are the seemingly more concrete considerations.

This attention to psychological balance has its counterpart on an institutional level, also. Within a school or school system, the critical balance between change and stability must always be kept in mind. Here again, this presupposes the kind of constant monitoring, both formal and informal, analytical and intuitive, that enables the head-teacher, Chief Education Officer or other change facilitator to gauge accurately the tenor of the collective frame of mind with regard to change. There is no hard and fast rule, but an intimate knowledge of the current state of the school, born of continual interaction and good instincts, can provide the necessary clues. Unquestionably, though, a school cannot tolerate too many elements in flux at one time. Attempting to address too great a number of purposes simultaneously may merely reduce the prospects for significant accomplishment for all of them. On the other hand, too narrow an approach may not produce sufficient magnitude of change to justify the effort required.

In the final analysis, what all of these perspectives on educational change seem to be pointing up is the need for informed guidance of the innovation process by headteachers or other change facilitators. Good judgement is surely a vital component of such effective leadership, and for school leaders attempting to improve their schools, this kind of balanced understanding of the various forces at work and their interrelationships would seem to be invaluable. Experience is doubtless a major factor in developing this ability, but to a certain extent, at least, it can also be taught. And one important way of doing so is by enhancing the practitioner's awareness of the subprocesses of change and their practical meaning in the school. Being thus alerted to potential problems, patterns of development and human responses to change, facilitators will be better equipped to respond in a

timely and effective manner and thereby to promote
the progression of change. Therefore, having hedged
sufficiently with regard to the limitations and
distortions inherent in our diagram and having also
considered some essential perspectives on change
that do not appear to be diagrammable, let us now
turn back to our partially discredited diagram of
change as we embark on a discussion of its respective subprocesses and their meaning for practitioners engaged in initiating or implementing an innovation. On behalf of those readers who may be dis-
turbed by the return to a tidy, rational, essentially linear presentation — for a circle, after all,
is merely a curved line — let me say that we do so
partly for want of a better method and partly out of
pure, unvarnished optimism. For if we are often
not, in practice, the rational beings we usually
pretend to be, we may at least engage our rational
faculties in the consideration of what our experience has shown us to be true and therefore useful,
whether rational or not.

A PRACTICAL ANATOMY OF CHANGE IN SCHOOLS

According to one rational progression, then, the
process of change includes a number of subprocesses
beginning with assessing current practice.

Assessment
A review of current practice is designed to illuminate the status quo within a given school or system
and in the process to call attention both to major
strengths and to areas in particular need of improvement. On this basis, informed choices may be
made that will have the most relevance for the
school. In the course of this kind of internal
assessment, a variety of measures are typically
employed. Student achievement test scores or
students' success on examinations may be employed as
a means of evaluating the effectiveness of current
education programmes. In addition to the strictly
curricular concerns, broader measures of school
climate and the various factors that affect it are
also considered. Included among these would be such
basic indicators as attendance and school stay-on
rate which could provide some useful clues concerning student morale and motivation. Naturally,
morale is an issue of vital importance for the
school as a whole, and in this connection attention

67

must also be paid to the prevailing attitudes and feelings of teachers, school management and parents.

Under various guises, the assessment concept, either as an ongoing part of regular school practice or within the more limited context of a particular innovation, has gained considerable currency in countries on both sides of the Atlantic. School Based Review (SBR) is particularly prevalent in the UK and Australia, and is also attracting increased attention in The Netherlands, Sweden and other European countries (Bollen & Hopkins, 1986; Hopkins, 1983). According to Van Velzen (1982), SBR is '...a systematic inspection (description and analysis) by a school, a sub-system or an individual (teacher, school leader) of the actual functioning of the school....' He goes on to state that '...it should always be the first step in a systematic school improvement process to gather diagnostic information in order to improve the functioning of the school' (p. 51). Thus, SBR is broadly viewed as a vital component of a rational approach to school change in the sense of improvement of existing practice as it impacts the achievement of educational objectives. Hopkins (1983, 1985) has provided a comprehensive overview of School Based Review, including methods of data collection, what aspects of school opera- tions to focus on and how to evaluate the data collected, as well as a valuable dual reference list which cites country-by-country project references in addition to a standard bibliography.

Various systematic approaches have been devel- oped in order to achieve the aims of School Based Review. In the UK, the Guidelines for Review and Institutional Development in Schools Project (GRIDS) (Bolam & McMahon, 1982; McMahon, 1982) is perhaps the foremost exponent of SBR. It is conceived as a one-year process encompassing five major stages: getting started, initial review, specific review, action for development, and overview and re-start. As the stages suggest, the project's purposes are two-fold: first, to review existing practice, and then to address those areas that have been identi- fied as priorities for improvement. Throughout the process, involvement of local school staff is crucial, and significant efforts are made to consult with them and otherwise maximise their commitment and participation. At the same time, the practical limits of the existing school situation with respect to time, money and personnel are recognised and the demands on staff are tailored to reflect those limits. In addition, external input and assistance are utilised when this seems appropriate (Bolam & McMahon, 1982; McMahon, 1982). A North American analogue to GRIDS is Blum's Goal-Based Education Program at Northwest Regional Educational Laboratory, which trains schools in viable self-improvement methods (Blum & Hord, 1983).

In its full-blown state, SBR is conceived as an innovation in its own right; specifically, the acquisition by both individuals and the school as a whole of certain 'meta-skills' that will enhance the total organisational capacity for problem solving (Runkel et al., 1979). In this way, school improvement as an open-ended, ongoing process may be fostered. But as Hopkins points out (1983), '...the ecology of the school militates against school based initiatives and tends to place other conflicting demands on the institution ...' (p. 4). Thus, in practice, the application of SBR in schools appears to be much less common than its theoretical significance would suggest, and where it is used, it is often within the more limited context of a specific innovation effort. The hope is, of course, that from this limited use a more general application of the process will evolve; but this transition is by no means automatic, and the requisite efforts to support it would constitute yet another set of demands on the key resources of the school.

In addition to these considerations, there is also the very real possibility that a particular innovation effort will not follow this balanced, rational course. As we have seen, many if not most innovations are externally mandated. Their appearance in the school may be attributed to a wide variety of interlocking factors, many of which may have little or nothing to do with the internal, local school situation. Under such circumstances, the concept of assessment, at least in its broader application, could have little relevance, except perhaps as a tool for de facto justification of a prior administrative decision. This qualification would apply equally to our next subprocess, exploring options. For if the decision to adopt an innovation arrives in the school as a fait accompli, there is obviously no room for consideration of other possibilities. Nevertheless, we now examine this subprocess, which is at least a possible, if somewhat idealised, component of change.

Exploring Options

Once a school or system has assessed its current practices and identified areas in need of improvement, the obvious question that arises is what do we do about it? In other words, is there an existing programme or process that could be purchased, acquired or learned that would address the identified need? Depending on the particular problem under consideration, the number of available options, and the time, money and desire for thoroughness the school has, the process of answering this question can easily take anywhere from six months to an entire year. The range of existing options could include both products offered by commercial publishers or educational consultants and individual programmes developed by other schools in response to a similar need that could be adapted for use. If, on the other hand, no such suitable programme or product can be found, or if the exploring school or system feels that its own situation is sufficiently unique to warrant it, a new curriculum or other programme or practice may be developed expressly to meet local needs.

As with the other subprocesses, the exploration of options can meaningfully be carried out at various levels, depending on the scope and focus of the proposed change. It may be the individual teacher seeking ways to enhance the learning process within a single classroom; then again, it may involve an entire school that wishes to institute school-wide change. On a still broader scale, the Chief Education Officer of an LEA might appoint a person or committee to undertake the task on behalf of all the affected schools. If the innovation in question is likely to affect a great many people, it may even be appropriate to initiate the exploration process on several levels simultaneously, in order to ensure maximum group input as a prerequisite to active involvement later on.

Assuming that a suitable existing programme were found and a decision to obtain it made, there would probably still be a need to adapt it to the school or system's specific situation. Here again, we are speaking in somewhat idealised terms, since time and resource limitations would necessarily place limits on the amount of preadoption activity that could be sustained. But, based on much experience it can certainly be said that those who are most effective in effecting change usually test the innovation in a pilot programme before introducing it into the entire system. This offers obvious advantages, as it enables the programme to be shaped to the particular user context in order to ensure a better institutional fit. Local context, of course, would include policy conflicts, resistance of staff to the change and other nonmaterial concerns that could have a major impact on the prospects for successful implementation. Prospective users might therefore do well to give serious consideration to this step, which in the long run could save far more time and trouble than it takes.

Having completed an assessment of current practice, identified the areas to be targeted for improvement and developed or discovered and tested appropriate innovations to address them, the time has then come to begin adoption.

Adoption

As we have seen, adoption is often, in practice, the real beginning of the innovation process, and certainly it is one subprocess that has been much scrutinised. Both researchers in their studies of change and theoreticians in their models have tended to devote a great deal of attention to adoption. This is understandable because, from a rational viewpoint, adoption does seem to constitute the pivotal point: someone makes a decision to start using the innovation and then innovation use begins. Of course, things are not usually either as logical or as simple as that, but in some sense this does seem to reflect what must happen. At some point, on some level, conscious choice is involved in the manifestation of a change in behaviour in most cases, at least the kind of broad and concrete institutional change we are considering here. Thus adoption is, unarguably, of vital importance to the innovation process. Unfortunately, what too often happens is that recognition of that importance comes at the expense of the attention paid to later, equally critical subprocesses.

Another reason for this perhaps excessive emphasis on adoption seems to be the inability of researchers and theoreticians to reach a consensus concerning just exactly what it is and is not. Often the concept of adoption spills over into initiation, and indeed, as we have tried to indicate by means of our self-replicating chain of diagrams, it is plainly impossible strictly and finally to define the line that separates the two subprocesses. Ultimately, of course, it does not really matter which categories are used to describe the change process, provided that nothing important gets left out. Adoption may be considered as a part of initiation, or vice versa, without necessarily doing damage to either one. But what should be stressed is that certain vital happenings need to be realised in order for the innovation process to unfold. Adoption in the sense of conscious choice is a prerequisite to effecting changes in practice, and after that choice has been made, a great many other things, which we may call initiation, need to happen in order for that decision to begin to be translated into action. As long as the attention paid to adoption does not cause us to lose sight of initiation, then, we will have no need to engage in fruitless semantic quarrels.

We have already seen how a subprocess such as exploring options can be carried out on a variety of levels, and this is even more applicable to adoption. At the systemwide level, the LEA may formally decide to adopt an innovation. At the school level, the school leadership and/or the school as a whole may make the decision to adopt; or, in the case of a much less widespread change, a faculty or department, or even an individual teacher may be doing the adopting. Adoption can happen successfully at any of these levels, as long as appropriate strategies and interventions are provided to support them. To a great extent, the ways that adoption happens necessarily reflect the existing authority structures within an institution or system, since these control the vital allocation of resources, both material and intangible (ie time and expertise). It is to be hoped, however, that those making the decision to adopt at higher levels will not do so without adequate input and feedback from the personnel who are to be affected by the change.

This brings us to perhaps the most important point. Essentially, adoption is in a very real sense an individual decision. Regardless of the level at which formal adoption takes place, in practice the decision to adopt an innovation must be made by every individual within the system. This is not to suggest that each person has carte blanche to accept or reject the change or that pressure and even outright coercion may not be used to secure those decisions. The institutional power structure and the particular interpersonal relationships within a given school will unquestionably affect the adoption subprocess in significant measure. Additionally, it would be naive to assume that every individual within a school could ever be encouraged,

persuaded or compelled to embrace wholeheartedly the
same innovation, however uncontroversial and effective it might appear to be. But, in relative terms,
the degree of acceptance or adoption of an innovation on the part of individuals has a considerable
bearing on its chances for successful implementation
and institutionalisation. Unquestionably, unless a
sizeable percentage of the affected individuals do
come to some positive accommodation with the
innovation, those chances will be almost nil. The
crucial consideration is that adoption represents
the first concrete step in people actually changing
their behaviour, which is the ultimate goal; and, as
such, its position in the innovation process is
critical indeed. As nearly as is possible in such
an imprecise arena, adoption marks the dividing line
between the preparatory subprocesses we have
previously considered and those that concern
themselves more directly with the alteration and
improvement of actual practice. It is the first of
these, initiation, to which we now turn.

Initiation
Whether it is labelled initiation, introduction,
mobilisation or whatever, this vital subprocess is
concerned with beginnings; that is, with getting
people motivated and mobilised, introducing the
innovation to them, describing it to them in ways
that are clear and reasonable and generally setting
in motion the process of transporting the prospective change from the realm of the theoretical to
that of the actual. The fact that we can still
speak of beginnings when we are already more or less
in the middle of our exposition of the change
process is just one more indication of the nonlinear, nondiscrete, overlapping nature of the
various subprocesses. In fact, the apparent
tenuousness of these subprocesses, or of their
boundaries at any rate, tends to increase rather
than diminish as the overall change continuum
progresses, because the 'earlier' subprocesses or
their effects are still resonating within the school
even as we move on to 'subsequent' ones.
    Unquestionably, the way the adoption subprocess
is handled can have tremendous significance for the
initiation and, by extension, implementation and
institutionalisation phases as well. As pointed
out, unless adoption in the sense of a decision to
'take on' the innovation occurs both on the formal
level in the school as a whole and more informally

within a substantial percentage of the affected individuals, all of the active subprocesses meant to follow it will be seriously jeopardised, and with them the long-term success of the innovation effort. But, particularly in the latter sense, adoption is likely to be a prolonged and continuing process of accretion and evolution of support that will still be going on through initiation and well into implementation. If the change is a small-scale, individual effort of only one or several teachers within a single school, then it is perhaps the headteacher or LEA who would need to be introduced to it carefully. But in the case of a mandated, top-down change, the roles would be reversed, with the higher and more centralised authorities trying to gain the interest, approval and active participation of teachers. Building commitment or 'ownership' of an innovation on the part of staff is a gradual, incremental undertaking; and indeed, one of the principal purposes of initiation is to foster the continued growth of that commitment or support. Realistically speaking, staff members as a body could scarcely be expected to muster a great deal of genuine enthusiasm and dedication concerning something they know almost nothing about, that initially appears to them in its most threatening aspect as a disrupter of the secure, established order and, most probably, a source of additional demands on their time. Rather, as Fullan (1985) has pointed out, for most teachers and administrators alike, familiarity and an increasing sense of comfort with an innovation will precede the formation of any deep commitment to it. Naturally there may be individuals whose greater enthusiasm for change in principle and higher tolerance for ambiguity in their work situation enable them to respond more positively to a proposed change from the outset. These are, of course, the very people whom an astute headteacher or other change facilitator will initially enlist in support of the innovation and I will have a good deal more to say about this in the following chapter.

As this discussion suggests, initiation and adoption are what might be termed twin subprocesses, or very near relations, at any rate. It is difficult to talk about one without repeated reference to the other. Thus, it is perhaps not surprising that there is so much disagreement among researchers on precisely where and how to draw the boundary line between the two subprocesses. Glatter, for example (forthcoming), defines 'introduction', his preferred term, broadly enough to encompass all of the subprocesses we have considered here so far. Fullan (1985) also broadly identifies a primary phase of the change process that may be called initiation; it is described as including mobilisation and as covering the period leading up to and including development and the decision to adopt, though it includes some of what could be described as occurring 'after' adoption had taken place, at least formally.

At any rate, my own observations of both the literature of change and actual school change efforts clearly suggest a very obvious trend of devoting far more attention to this whole overlapping area of change than to the succeeding or following subprocesses. This merely confirms the almost instinctual human tendency to conceptualise and to invest the beginnings and the ends of things with far more significance than what lies in between. Births and deaths, whether of individuals or organisations or projects such as educational innovations, usually attract far more fanfare and notice than the same subjects may during their effective lifetimes. Thus, when the decision to begin an innovation has been taken, it is often accompanied by excitement and activity or even celebration. Unfortunately, it is not the short-term burst of enthusiasm but rather the slow, plodding, day-to-day support that determines an innovation's ultimate success or failure and, too often, this is a commodity in woefully short supply. We saw in Chapter Two how quickly and precipitously the amount of attention in most theoretical models of change drops off following adoption, and my research in schools and discussions with school leaders in many countries have confirmed that, in practice, few of them pay much attention to the post-adoption subprocesses, either. It is, in fact, one of the principal purposes of this book to illuminate the 'subprocess in the middle' of change and to stress its vital significance.

This is not in any way to undermine the importance of the adoption/initiation package, however. To quote Glatter (forthcoming) again:

> Although much research shows that the components of implementation and integration need close attention if successful change is to be achieved...and there has too often been an assumption that you only need to introduce an innovation for it to be effectively absorbed by

the institution, we must not ignore introduction because subsequent problems may often be directly traceable to what was done, or not done, at the time of introduction. The idea may not even survive beyond the introductory component.

Unquestionably, then, we may conclude that initiation represents another vital perspective on the change process, one that neither practitioners nor theoreticians can afford to overlook. At the same time, to overemphasise it could prove equally disastrous. If we were to attempt another formulation, based on this discussion, it might look like this: INITIATION = ADOPTION + MOBILISATION. But it must always be kept clearly in mind that these are interlocking puzzle pieces whose coherence can ultimately only be derived from the total picture to which they all contribute. In this light, we may now proceed to a consideration of our next subprocess, implementation.

Implementation

In the past, neither theoretician nor practitioner paid much attention to implementation. Indeed, in many instances it was not even recognised as a distinct entity deserving of attention. However, the repeated failures of cleverly designed and enthusiastically adopted innovation packages virtually forced concerned educators to look beyond the adoption/initiation point in their quest for answers to the puzzle of the change process. Thus, implementation began to attract the interest of researchers and to appear more frequently in the literature. This led to a greater appreciation of the crucial importance of this 'process in the middle' of change and also to some reformulation of the early change models which, as we have seen, did not generally have much to say about it. Even so, it was only very slowly and perhaps even reluctantly that this concern began spilling over into the practical arena. In the last few years, an increasing number of school leaders and other educators have started recognising that implementation is a serious business requiring considerable planning, nurturing and active involvement if it is to be successfully realised.

Part of the reason for this lag may be that implementation represents the point at which school leaders and other change facilitators can begin to exert a major influence on the course of the change process within their schools. As such, it can substantially affect their day-to-day behaviour in concrete, immediate ways. To a lesser extent, the same could be said about initiation, except that the usual time frame involved is vastly different. Adoption and initiation may be accomplished fairly rapidly; this is not to say that they should be hastily carried out without careful consideration, or that certain aspects of these subprocesses may not extend over more considerable periods of time. But the formal decision to adopt an innovation, at least, need not require a great deal of time and initiation can likewise be launched relatively quickly. Implementation, on the other hand, is an extremely lengthy process. A minimum of several years is needed for even the simplest, least complex or problematical innovation to be implemented. This is a hard but vital lesson for us all, one that has come slowly out of many years of research and practical experience, not all of it positive.

Implementation, then, is at once the source of great opportunities and substantial challenges, and the reasons behind both of these are rooted in the nature of this subprocess. During implementation, teachers and others involved in an innovation are learning about it, discovering how to use it, assimilating its intricacies and becoming efficient and comfortable with its use in their classrooms. In other words, they are seeking to master the innovation, and mastery will obviously take far longer than the kind of superficial acquaintance initiation can provide. The clear prerequisite for mastery is hands-on, practical experience, for which there is no substitute; and in most cases, this will inevitably include a certain amount of fumbling and stumbling around until sufficient expertise is achieved. In addition, it is during implementation that most of the problems connected with an innovation will first become glaringly apparent. These would include both built-in problems attributable to the programme's design and the resistances, conflicts and other difficulties stemming from the interpersonal problems and concerns of individual staff members.

For all of these reasons, then, implementation is also perhaps the likeliest point at which the innovation process breaks down. Effectively confronting and managing such a range of problems over such a considerable period of time can be a formidable task and certainly one not likely to be achieved by accident. In many instances, it is the innovation itself that is perceived to be at fault when it fails to take hold and we may never know how many perfectly serviceable programmes have been prematurely scrapped simply because inadequate measures were taken to ensure their implementation. Even more than some of the other subprocesses, implementation might be characterised as an invisible entity. Like 'black holes', whose existence can be detected only by noting the perturbative effects their gravitational fields have on neighbouring stars, implementation is in a sense most conspicuous in its influence on the course of the entire innovation process and the ultimate presence or absence of institutionalisation. In retrospect, at least, as researchers have gradually come to understand, a lack of sufficient attention to implementation may be strongly suspected whenever an innovation adopted and launched with appropriate fanfare and apparent support simply belly ups and dies, taking with it the optimistic efforts and hopes of those who tried to make it happen.

To speak of retrospection may be fine for theoreticians, but practitioners must usually remain more firmly centred in the here and now, and de facto explanations as to what went wrong may seem to be of little use to them. Fortunately, the lessons of hindsight can support tomorrow's foresight; we now have a clear and specific idea of the functions that need to be realised in order for significant and lasting change to occur (Hord & Huling-Austin, 1986). A key point to consider here, though, is that <u>someone has to do these things</u>: monitoring, providing feedback and logistical support and the effective use of authority to sanction the change can all have vital impact, but they will not simply happen of their own accord. Rather, it will require the concerted and continued efforts of a number of committed, adequately prepared individuals. And for headteachers or other internal change facilitators, this may necessitate a fundamental re-evaluation of their role within the school. I will have a good deal more to say about change facilitators and their particular concerns in the next chapter.

Throughout this discussion, I have taken special pains to avoid conveying the impression that change is a linear process, with discrete components neatly following each other in predictable succession. But there is at least one aspect of change that does readily admit a causal, linear interpretation, or at least a kind of negative causality. If

it is misleading to assume or imply that these
successive steps lead neatly (or at all) to institutionalisation, it is indisputable that the absence
of key subprocesses can effectively prevent it. The
lack of adoption on one or more levels obviously
precludes any further movement with an innovation.
Perhaps more subtly, and therefore significantly,
lack of adequate implementation all but assures the
failure of institutionalisation. Thus, a continuing
appreciation both of the respective subprocesses and
their interconnections is necessary if change is to
be managed successfully and seen through to its
objective. As far as boundaries are concerned, we
have no more idea where implementation begins and
ends than with any of the other subprocesses; they
all are part of an ongoing movement or activity
sequence that helps support people in their change.
The progression of initiation helps generate the
deeper involvement and commitment of implementation
and, at some point, implementation blends into, and
becomes, institutionalisation.

Institutionalisation and Beyond
Looking back over the course of a 'completed'
innovation effort, the change process might be
visualised as a kind of wave function, with a small
and somewhat narrow beginning that rises during
adoption and initiation, peaks in implementation,
and subsides or tapers into institutionalisation at
the other end. What such a graph would really be
measuring would be the degree of disruption connected with the change. Its subsidence at the further
limit does not indicate any diminishing of the
change itself (on the contrary, it is at this point
that the change becomes truly effective in practice), but rather of the disruption and uncertainty
that are at once the inevitable companions and the
principal defeaters of change. Institutionalisation, then, is in one sense a point of arrival for
the implementation journey, which is continued until
this point is reached and, hopefully, beyond. To
subvert the metaphor a moment, we might visualise
change as a solitary trekker negotiating a ridgeline
trail who, from the peak of institutionalisation,
can effectively survey the previously covered
terrain and take stock of what has been achieved,
before proceeding down again and onward toward the
next great height.
    The recent flowering of interest in implementa-
tion has naturally spilled over into institutional-

isation as well and the prior lack of mention of it
in the literature is quickly being rectified. This
was confirmed by a June 1985 conference in Lucerne,
at which scholars from many countries shared their
views   and   findings   about   institutionalisation.
Among the various approaches to their subject taken
by these researchers, some fundamental distinctions
may be discerned.   Most of the conceptualisation of
institutionalisation has concentrated on one of two
main concerns: how do you make it happen, and how
do you determine if and when it has, in fact,
occurred (Van Hees, forthcoming).   In the attempts
to answer these questions, attention has tended to
be focused on either the individual or the organisation as a unit of measure.

Miles (1983) has made a major contribution to
our   understanding   of   institutionalisation   as   an
organisational phenomenon.   Drawing on the work of
Yin and others (1978), Miles identifies various
benchmarks for determining if institutionalisation
has been achieved; these are grouped under the
rubrics Passage Completion and Cycle Survival.
Included in the former group would be, in the USA,
the change from soft to hard money for funding the
innovation,   standardisation   of   job   descriptions
including the new responsibilities or skills and
establishment of routines for supply and maintenance.   Examples of Cycle Survival would be survival
of   annual   budget   cycles,   survival   of   personnel
changes and the teaching of requisite skills in
successive cycles.   According to this view, if the
innovation's current status meets these and other
related criteria, then institutionalisation has
occurred within the organisation.

Miles   also   addresses   the   question   of   how
schools may reach this desired state of affairs;
that is, what strategies or factors are useful or
necessary   in   achieving   institutionalisation.
Various considerations are cited, including administrative commitment and support, assistance for new
users and sufficient user effort.   In addition,
contextual factors such as stability of programme
staff and (especially) leadership, environmental
balance and career advancement motivation are
acknowledged.   In Miles' view, when these organisational structures and objectives are in place, the
prospects for institutionalisation will be extremely
favourable.   But he stresses that the realisation of
the   structures,   and   thus   institutionalisation
itself,   depends   on   another   vital   factor—

administrative pressure. When heads or other change facilitators lend the full weight of their authority to an innovation, and thus put pressure on their teachers to adopt it, greater frequency of use results. And this, together with provision of adequate user assistance and other requisite factors, leads in turn to increased user commitment, a key hallmark of successful implementation (Miles, 1983). To bring this conception more closely in alignment with the present discussion, we could say that change within a school begins with a strong administrative commitment to an innovation (adoption). The administrator(s) then provide support and pressure on its behalf (initiation) and encourage and assist their staff in using it (implementation). As a result of all of this activity, stabilised, regular use is achieved (institutionalisation).

The importance of administrative pressure is also emphasised by other writers. Hord and Hall (1986) approach institutionalisation from a completely different standpoint; instead of looking at the organisation, they focus on the individual, concluding that when each individual has achieved institutionalisation, then the organisation as a whole will have done so, and not before. This viewpoint is supported by the work of Fullan and Park (1981), who also stress the primacy of the human over the material component in innovation. Nevertheless, they too affirm the necessity of pressure as a prelude to realising significant change. To state it simply: SUPPORT + PRESSURE = CHANGE. Like most neat slogans, of course, this one encompasses a world of complexity, and realising and maintaining the delicate yet crucial balance between the humanitarian concerns of supportive behaviour and the pragmatic dictates of responsible authority could be fairly said to constitute the fundamental practical problem of change management.

The individual approach to institutionalisation looks at users of an innovation--their feelings, attitudes and behaviours--as the basis for determining its status in the school. This approach will be explored in far greater detail in Part Two of this book, in connection with the techniques and problems of innovation monitoring; but for the moment we may broadly identify three principal user-related variables for gauging individual change. These are teachers' feelings about the innovation, their behaviours with it and the form or shape their use takes in practice, compared to the original intention or design. When teachers, on the strength of sufficient experience, are no longer concerned with the logistics of innovation use; when their behaviour with respect to the innovation is organised and made routine so that they can shift their attention to their students' behaviour with it; and when the innovation in practice assumes a form that is compatible with the original intention, then we may confidently say that, for those individuals, at least, institutionalisation has indeed occurred.

This assessment appears valid as long as we view institutionalisation solely from a three-dimensional perspective: that is, as a particular target or point in time to be reached. But if we see it as a subprocess unfolding over time, there is a final and perhaps even more fundamental factor that needs to be recognised. If we define institutionalisation (to cull a few examples from the literature) as 'continuation' (Berman & McLaughlin, 1978), 'integration' (Van Hees, forthcoming) or 'built-in-ness' (Miles, 1983), then the key test would be: does innovation use continue? Thus, we may further refine our definition as follows: Institutionalisation means that users have reached a particular point or degree of assimilation of an innovation and then continue using it; and in this formulation, we would stress that both factors are equally important. If the users are still tentative, disorganised or patently frantic with the innovation, then clearly it is not being used well and implementation has not yet been realised, much less institutionalisation. If, on the other hand, innovation use is well established in the classroom and the new programme or approach is being used 'robustly' in a coordinated, organised and meaningful way with students, then implementation, at least, has been achieved. But if, as all too often happens, the innovation abruptly disappears from the classroom the following year, then institutionalisation was obviously not accomplished. Only if such use continues over time can we legitimately recognise institutionalisation. To put it simply, implementation is the process of attaining this 'good use' and institutionalisation denotes its continuation in practice within the institution.

WHERE DO WE GO FROM HERE?

The foregoing discussion of the change process as it actually appears in schools has attempted to represent accurately and thoroughly the realities as I understand them. Inevitably, however, certain distortions will have crept in. Despite all my protestations about the limitations and oversimplifications of diagrams and models, I have presented them. And my assertions of the nonlinear character of change notwithstanding, I have proceeded to present an essentially linear categorisation of subprocesses that inherently suggests, at least, a progression of discrete stages leading to a precise and incontrovertible terminal point. This may be unavoidable, given the essentially objective orientation of our thought processes; but the stubborn refusal of real events to behave 'as they should' by conforming to our limited conceptualisations provides a constant reminder that we must always strive to look beyond them.

The plain fact, as both research and practical experience have amply confirmed, is that no theoretical programme for change or identified succession of stages can by itself represent accurately and thoroughly the actual appearances of all real change efforts in practice, much less guarantee the achievement of tangible practical success. It is entirely possible for a change to have apparently gone through all the subprocesses and be in widespread and effective use and still simply to fade away within the next year. Berman and McLaughlin (1978) have shown that government-funded programmes, at least in the USA, tend not to be continued once the special funding stops; and Miles (1983) points out the potentially fatal effect on an innovation of the departure from a school or system of an innovation's major advocate. These examples illustrate the crucial difference between superficial acceptance of a change and what Miles calls 'built-in-ness'. But, having distinguished them in theory, how do we, short of waiting for the innovation to succeed or fail and drawing retrospective conclusions, do so in practice?

Two major points suggest themselves. The first is that we cannot afford the luxury of a strictly linear, causal approach to change; rather, the 'earlier' subprocesses must be continued even after the 'achievement' of institutionalisation. The administrative sanctioning and support for the innovation that characterised its adoption must be

carried forward to ensure its continued legitimacy
in the eyes of staff members. For new teachers
subsequently joining the staff, the same informational and technical assistance that accompanied the
original initiation must be provided. And certainly, the active logistical support, classroom monitoring, and feedback typical of an effective implementation effort need to be continued by some
member(s) of the change team to help ensure continued use of the innovation in acceptable form. As we
have seen, however, even all of this is not necessarily enough. The second point, therefore, is that
institutionalisation in the sense of ensured,
continued, long-term use has its own programme of
requisite actions that need to be pursued every bit
as actively as those done in support of the other
subprocesses. No innovation will get permanently
funded or incorporated into teachers' job descriptions merely by accident, and the same can be said
for widespread, comfortable, effective classroom
use. Headteachers and other administrators in
particular will need to take note of this point and
its practical implications for their work in
schools, which will be considered further in subsequent chapters.

Finally, however, even if all of the above is
dutifully and thoroughly carried out, there remains
an additional point that needs to be made. Any
innovation, regardless of how 'good' it is and how
effectively it has been implemented and institutionalised, will ultimately still need to be changed
again. For change is an open-ended process; it has
no express or definitive conclusion. To return to
our earlier metaphor, the solitary trekker, on
conquering the next peak, once again surveys the
newly augmented expanse of terrain just covered and
from the substantially changed perspective of this
current vantage point and the new information it
provides, may make a different assessment of present
circumstances. But this changed conception will be
no more definitive or permanent than its predeces-
sor; rather, it too will be replaced as soon as
further progress or experience sheds a different
light on things. A ridgeline trail is really
nothing but a series of peaks and cols to be ascend-
ed, descended and traversed and this successive,
progressive, up-and-down movement over unfamiliar,
changing terrain may perhaps most aptly characterise
the fluid, evolutionary face of change. As Miles
(1983), discussing data from the site of a successfully implemented change effort, puts it: 'The

ultimate measure of institutionalisation at Tindale, ironically enough, appears in this sentence: "In several years, it will be revised, just as all other curricula are revised on a regular basis"' (page 17). This need not be taken by practitioners as an occasion for tearing out of hair and bemoaning the futility of all their labours, however. Ultimately, recognition that this kind of ongoing, open-ended improvement is not merely an acceptable but indeed a truly desirable process is, in fact, the key to opening whole new vistas of potential educational innovation.

It is hoped that this discussion in these first three chapters, of the history of educational change, its variously imagined theoretical formulations and some common patterns of behaviour that may be expected to accompany it in practice, will have helped readers broaden their understanding and appreciation of the change process and its complexities, problems and rewards. But for practitioners, at least, the fundamental question remains: now that we know _about_ it, how do we _do_ it? In Part Two of this volume, we will explore in depth a concrete, practical, battle-tested methodology for evaluating and managing educational innovation.

REFERENCES

Berman, P., & McLaughlin, M. (1978). Federal programs supporting educational change, Vol. VIII: Implementing and sustaining innovations. Santa Monica, CA: Rand Corporation.

Blum, R.E., & Hord, S.M. (1983) Using research as a basis for school improvement in Alaska. The Journal of Staff Development, 4 (1), 136-151.

Bolam, R., & McMahon, A. (1982). Guidelines for review and institutional development in schools (GRIDS) project: Interim report. University of Bristol/Schools Council.

Bollen, R. & Hopkins, D. (1986). School based review: Towards a praxis. Leuven, Belgium: ACCO.

Fullan, M. (1982). The meaning of educational change. New York: Teachers College Press.

Fullan, M. (1985). Change processes and strategies at the local level. The Elementary School Journal, 85 (3), 391-421.

Fullan, M., & Park, P. (1981). Curriculum implementation: A resource guide. Toronto: Ontario Ministry of Education.

Glatter, R. (forthcoming). The role of school leaders in the introduction of school improvement. In E. Stego, K. Gielen, R. Glatter, & S. Hord (Eds.). The role of school leaders in school improvement. Leuven, Belgium: Acco.

Hopkins, D. (1983). School based review for school improvement: A preliminary state of the art. Paris: Organisation for Economic Co-operation and Development/Centre for Educational Research and Innovation.

Hopkins, D. (1985). School based review for school improvement. Leuven/Amersfoort: Acco.

Hord, S.M., & Hall, G.E. (1986). Institutionalization of innovations: Knowing when you have it and when you don't. Paper presented at the annual meeting of the American Educational Research Association, San Francisco.

Hord, S.M. & Huling-Austin, L. (1986). Effective curriculum implementation: Some promising new insights. The Elementary School Journal, 87 (1), 97-115.

McMahon, A. (1982). The GRIDS project. Educational Management and Administration, 10 (3), 217-221.

Miles, M. (1983). Unraveling the mystery of institutionalization. Educational Leadership, 41 (3), 14-19.

Runkel, P.J., Schmuck, R.A., Arends, J.H., & Francisco, R.P. (1979). Transforming the school's capacity for problem solving. Eugene, OR: Centre for Educational Policy and Management.

Rutherford, W., & Murphy, S. (1985). Change in high schools: Roles and reactions of teachers. Paper presented at the annual meeting of the American Educational Research Association, Chicago.

Vandenberghe, R. (1982). Renewed primary school in Belgium. Leuven, Belgium: Katholieke Universiteit.

Van Hees, T. (forthcoming). Institutionalization and the school's capacity to change. In E. Stego, K. Gielen, R. Glatter, & S. Hord (Eds.). The role of school leaders in school improvement. Leuven, Belgium: Acco.

Van Velzen, W.G. (1982). <u>Conceptual mapping of school improvement</u>. Paris: Organisation for Economic Co-operation and Development/Centre for Educational Research and Innovation.

Yin, R. Quick, S., Bateman, P., & Marks, E. (1978). <u>Changing urban bureaucracies: How new practices become routinized</u>. Santa Monica, CA: Rand Corporation.

Part Two

TOOLS FOR CHANGE

Chapter 4

ASSESSING CHANGE: CURRENT STATUS, CREEDS AND NEEDS

Part One has provided a variety of differing perspectives on educational innovation, based on many
years of research and experience. I have talked a
great deal about the concept of change as a process
and about change as the focus of one or another
model, programme or theory. We have examined the
history of efforts to improve schools, seeking in
that motley and often discouraging compendium of
noble intentions, bright hopes and misconstrued or
prematurely discarded programmes some useful clues
concerning what change is and how we make it happen.
Finally, in Chapter Three, we attempted to describe
how the change process looks, not within the orderly
and unencumbered pages of books but in the busy,
boisterous classrooms and corridors of real schools.
We have thus moved gradually away from abstraction
and toward the concrete realities of schools and
school leaders.
        But all of these perspectives, though useful,
fall short of offering the practitioner specific
tools and methods for applying their lessons to the
needs and complications of specific situations in
schools. How do we recognise in practice just what
is happening with a given innovation in our school?
And having done so, what do we do about it? Part
One of this book has given ample illustration of the
evident fact that introduction without implementation does not yield effective or lasting innovation.
And as our historical survey of change efforts and
approaches in Chapter One shows, lack of understanding of the process of change and its meaning for
schools was frequently a major impediment to the
achievement of real change. When, therefore,
researchers became aware of this lack of knowledge
about the change process, they began to shift their
focus more and more from innovation product to

process, and thus to accumulate the data base from which our subsequent, improved understanding could be formed.

THE CONCERNS-BASED APPROACH

In the United States, as we have noted, The Research and Development Center for Teacher Education at The University of Texas at Austin was among the major research facilities involved in the study of change in schools. As a result of many years of intensive, school-based research, the Concerns-Based Adoption Model (CBAM), which is described in detail in the following pages, was developed. It consists of a series of ideas, methods and measurements that, taken together, comprise a practical, effective answer to the dilemma of practitioners confronting or managing educational change. Both solidly grounded in careful research and extensively tested in real-life applications, CBAM draws on many of the perspectives we have explored in prior chapters, making use of their rich insights while attempting to avoid their pitfalls.

Our brief guided tours of the history of change in schools, its theoretical formulations and actual appearance, then, have not been merely interesting diversions en route to our main thesis. Rather, they have contributed significantly to evolving the essential philosophical underpinnings of the system I now describe. It is, in fact, as much the failed innovation efforts of the past as the successes that, together with the imagination, vision and experience of innumerable researchers and practitioners, have provided the conceptual basis for what follows. And undoubtedly the firm, pragmatic base of the CBAM approach has much to do with its broad applicability and practical utility to those engaged in implementing change in schools.

From this richly varied body of research, observation and experience, certain fundamental assumptions have been distilled and, since they are the foundation which supports the whole theoretical and practical structure, a clear understanding of what they are and what they mean is crucial to a full appreciation of the model and its uses. Before we proceed to examine the components of the system, therefore, it will be useful to discuss these underlying assumptions and their impact on what follows.

Assumptions Underlying CBAM Research

The Concerns-Based Adoption Model (Hall, Wallace & Dossett, 1973) is an empirically-based conceptual framework which outlines the developmental process that individuals experience as they implement an innovation. The CBAM evolved out of extensive research on the change process as a whole, with special emphasis on the implementation of educational innovations in North American schools and colleges. This research gave birth to seven basic assumptions about change and how it can best be facilitated; these assumptions have informed and guided the model's development.

Change is a process, not an event. One of the most ubiquitous, persistent obstructions to successful innovation is the tendency conceptually to objectify change, making it an object or event of discrete, identifiable dimensions rather than an intangible, ongoing, multidimensional process involving many sources, variables and participants. This tendency is unfortunately reinforced by the practical demands of daily life with its deadlines, conflicting priorities that vie for attention, and pressures to produce 'results'. In addition, the anxieties and added stress typically experienced by individuals confronting change provide further support for this behaviour by promoting a strong desire to 'get it over with' and thereby to reduce the stress, as if change were a specific point in time that could be reached and passed by. All these trends, however, serve severely to limit the possibilities and permissible scope of change efforts. Thus, recognition that change is a process occurring over time, and by this is meant, usually, a period of years, is an essential prerequisite to its successful implementation.

Change is made by individuals first. Another common tendency in approaching change is to consider it in broad, impersonal terms, as a package or programme affecting many people yet distinct from all of them. This approach would obviously appeal to both programme developers and high level administrators or legislators, for whom it would at least appear to simplify the sometimes thorny questions surrounding adoption and implementation. But close examination reveals it to be a contradiction in terms; for if change does, indeed, affect many people, it can not be completely distinct from them. And if change is, as we have suggested, a process occurring over time, then the reactions and adjustments of the affected individuals must constitute an essential part of that continuum of growth. Individuals, in fact, must be the primary focus of actions taken to promote change, since the active, appropriate, sustained participation of enough of them is what distinguishes a programme on paper from a meaningful and fully realised one in practice. Only when a sufficient number of individuals have genuinely embraced and absorbed a change can it truly be said that the institution or system to which they belong has changed.

Change is a highly personal experience. This might seem to be such a logical corollary to the last point as not even to need stating; but the key point here is individual differentiation. Too often, individuals may be viewed as a numerical assemblage of largely interchangeable units, with little allowance made for differences in how they will respond. Though they are approached individually, they are expected to behave, in effect, collectively. This approach does grave injustice to the staggering diversity and alternately wonderful and maddening unpredictability of human behaviour; it also seriously undermines the likelihood of successful implementation. The fact is that each individual reacts significantly differently to change, in accordance with a plethora of highly personalised factors. As Rogers and Shoemaker have pointed out (1971), these responses can to some extent be categorised as an aid to understanding and preparing for them; but failure to take sufficient account of the differences, which will almost certainly include discrepancies from the expected tidy categories, can only inhibit the progress of initiation and implementation of change.

Change entails multilevel developmental growth. Even within an individual, change is not a totally coherent, rational, unitary function. Rather, what we label 'change' is an irregular assemblage of emotional, intellectual and behavioural responses that affect the individual and thus, the school, in a variety of ways. Speaking broadly, these may be grouped under 'feelings' and 'skills', and progressive alteration in both these areas is essential to the accomplishment of real change. Our previous emphasis on change as process applies equally here, however; and these shifts in feelings and skills are also processes that subtly and gradually unfold. During this process, though, there are identifiable 'stages' of feeling and 'levels' of skill with respect to the innovation that individuals pass through as part of their experience of change over time. In the following pages, we will consider these stages and levels in detail and discuss how to recognise and measure them in practice, for they can be invaluable tools for school leaders and other change facilitators to use in evaluating and managing change.

Change is best understood in operational terms. Nowhere is the gap between theoretician and practitioner more glaringly apparent or more potentially problematic than in the introduction of innovations into schools. Too often, innovation packages conceived by developers in abstract conceptual terms are presented to practitioners in ways that may seem totally alien to their world of concrete, practical concerns. Both the terminology and overall approach to schools employed by theoreticians may be unfamiliar to teachers and other intended users of an innovation and, thus, can critically interfere with its implementation. For most individual practitioners, therefore, change will be best understood if it is presented or described to them in operational terms, as it would appear when fully in use. In other words, teachers encountering a new programme will naturally relate to it in terms of what it will mean or do to their current classroom practice. What changes in behaviour, whether theirs or their students', will it require? What additional skills will need to be acquired? How much preparation time will be needed? By addressing these concrete, immediate practitioner concerns, change facilitators can at once improve communication and reduce individual resistance to change.

Change facilitation must suit individual needs. Actions taken to promote the implementation and institutionalisation of change are most likely to succeed insofar as they are geared to the diagnosed needs of individual users. If change is perceived as taking place within individuals in a variety of ways, then clearly different responses and

interventions will be appropriate to different
individuals. A client-centred diagnostic model such
as CBAM, which can pinpoint and describe the special
needs and problems of individual users, can provide
vital assistance to the change facilitator in taking
appropriate actions. At the same time, the client
also benefits by receiving timely and appropriate
personalised attention. Thus, this approach to
implementing change can help to maximise the prospects for success while minimising the severity of
individual problems with the innovation.

Change efforts should focus on individuals, not
innovations. Just as we tend to objectify change as
a discrete event, so we also tend to see it mainly
in terms of the innovation package, a concrete
object we can hold in our hand. To do this, however, is to forget that books and charts and papers
alone do not make change; only people can make
change, by appropriately altering their behaviour.
Ultimately, the real meaning and value of any
innovation lies in its human, not its material
component. But even scrupulous attention to the
needs of individuals will not be enough if it is
conceived, in totality, as a process of adapting
them to fit the existing innovation. Rather,
effective change facilitators work in an adap-
tive/systemic fashion, tailoring their interventions
to the needs of clients within the change and, as
appropriate and necessary, tailoring the preconceived form of the change itself to the problems and
needs of the local system. Systemic functioning
also implies recognition that the school as a whole
will be affected by whatever is done with respect to
even its smallest part, and interventions in one
area may well produce unexpected results in another.
Thus, preconceived ideas about the speed with which
implementation can be achieved, the specific actions
needed to achieve it, and even the form that the
implemented programme will ultimately take may well
have to be altered or set aside. Otherwise, they
may become not aids but impediments to successful
realisation of change.

DIAGNOSTIC DIMENSIONS OF THE CBAM

Based on the perspective framed by these assumptions
and tested during more than a decade of school-based
research, the CBAM programme has developed and

refined a set of conceptual tools for planning, facilitating, monitoring and evaluating change in schools. There are four main components within the model: Stages of Concern, Levels of Use, Innovation Configurations and Intervention Taxonomy. Each of them may be conceived as addressing a different dimension of change; together they comprise a comprehensive practical approach to implementing innovations and evaluating their use. In the following pages, we will consider each of them in turn, explaining its meaning and exploring its implications and practical value to school leaders and other change facilitators.

Stages of Concern

Stages of Concern (SoC) may be aptly characterised as the cornerstone of the whole CBAM model. In theory, SoC is a fundamental conceptual tool for approaching innovation of whatever sort; in practice, it is a valuable technique for information gathering and for formative evaluation of innovation use. In fact, all of the CBAM-related work on assessing and facilitating the innovation process, and thus, the promotion of productive, positive and lasting change, is firmly grounded in the theory and practice of SoC. It seems appropriate, therefore, to consider briefly the origins and development of this vital tool.

Roots of SoC.
Stages of Concern had its beginnings at least three decades ago. It is a concept that has developed gradually in the course of many years of research and development, deriving much from prior work. A good place to start in explaining SoC is with the work of Gabriel in the 1950s. Gabriel conducted a study of two groups of teachers, beginner and experienced, in terms of their work-related problems and satisfactions (1957). What Gabriel uncovered was a fundamental difference in teachers' perceptions and overall outlook, based on their experience. For beginner teachers, the biggest problems identified were criticism by superiors and student discipline; correspondingly, their greatest satisfactions were praise by supervisors and holidays. For more experienced teachers, however, the picture was essentially different. Their biggest problem was the slow progress of certain pupils and their greatest satisfaction, naturally enough, was observing the success of former pupils. Both of

these responses are markedly student focused, in contrast to the far more immediate personal orientation of their less experienced colleagues. The difference in their situations, then, prompted a widely varying outlook on their work.

The next major step in the evolution of a concerns-based approach came with the work of Frances Fuller in the USA. Armed with a grant from the National Institute of Mental Health, Fuller sought to make as broad an impact as possible on education in the USA. She hypothesised that if we could find ways to promote the emotional maturity and mental health of elementary school teachers, it could have a powerful effect on the whole education system, both immediately and in the longer term.

One experience that significantly altered the direction of Fuller's thought and work came when she was teaching an undergraduate educational psychology class. She customarily solicited feedback from students and, for this course, 97 of 100 students called her course irrelevant. Undaunted but intrigued, she examined the backgrounds of the three who had not concurred with the overwhelming majority of their classmates, and found that, in contrast to the others, these students had all had prior experience working with children, either in Sunday School, summer camp or elsewhere. They therefore already had firsthand knowledge about children and how to interact with them which, as Gabriel had shown, gave them a substantially different perspective on students and teaching. Encouraged by this experience, Fuller began studying the concerns of pre-service teachers as they were about to begin student teaching. She noticed that most pre-service teacher preparation programmes seemed to be seriously out of synch with the way these teacher candidates were thinking about their new profession. Obviously, such a gap could significantly reduce the programmes' effectiveness. Based on this work, Fuller developed what she called the concept of Teachers' Concerns (1969), which she used as a way of organising teacher preparation courses and materials to make them more relevant to students.

Before they began student teaching, Fuller found that, for the most part, students were far more concerned with their social lives or other personal matters than with anything related to their work. As soon as they were introduced to the idea of the student teaching practicum, however, these <u>unrelated concerns</u> underwent an immediate and drastic change, converting rapidly to <u>self concerns</u>:

will my supervising teacher like me? will the head accept me? where will I park my car? and so on. Even though these students had yet to begin student teaching, the idea of it had changed from a nebulous abstraction to an imminent and threatening reality impinging on their lives. Once they began student teaching and had an opportunity to confront and resolve some of these self concerns, their attention increasingly shifted to logistical problems, which Fuller labelled <u>task concerns</u>: where are the books? where is paper kept? how do I make daily lesson plans? and the like. Essentially, all of these concerns boil down to simply getting the job done and getting through the day. For many student teachers, preoccupation with these concerns marked the limit of their growth; about two-thirds of them never moved beyond task concerns during student teaching. Experienced teachers, on the other hand, were far more likely, eventually, to achieve a level of operational self-confidence sufficient to enable them to direct more of their energy toward <u>impact concerns</u>. These focus not on the teacher, as do self and task concerns, but on the students, specifically on what effect the teacher's efforts have on them. Ideally, of course, this would be the focus of all teaching activity. But realistically speaking, as the work of Gabriel and Fuller and much subsequent research have shown, this operational level cannot be reached until and unless the prior concerns have been adequately dealt with. And, indeed, even among experienced teachers, many never reach the stage of impact concerns.

As we have noted, Fuller applied her results to the reconsideration and redesign of teacher preparation programmes and materials, seeking to make them more relevant to the real concerns of student teachers and therefore, more effective proving grounds (1973). But the implications of a concerns-based approach are far reaching, embracing a great many other possibilities as well. Stages of Concern, which takes Fuller's work as a point of departure, explores some of the diagnostic, change-related uses of this concept.

<u>Seven Graded Stages</u>. Stages of Concern, then, is an elaborated set of categories denoting an individual's theoretical or actual progression with respect to an innovation. In the place of Gabriel's two categories or Fuller's four, however, SoC employs seven numbered stages in order to provide a more

detailed and useful picture of the specific state of
each individual's, and by extension, the whole
group's, concerns about an innovation at a given
point in time (Hall & Rutherford, 1976). These
stages, matched with typical expressions of concern
and correlated with Fuller's categories, are summarised in Figure 4.1. It should be noted that, for
the purposes of our discussion, 'innovation' is
conceived as anything that is new to an individual.
Thus, what is an innovation for one person may not
be for another in the same school. This may seem
confusing to readers accustomed to a more generalised institutional viewpoint. But SoC is primarily a measure of individuals' affective responses,
which tend to be strongest during confrontations
with the new and alien. And the key to concerns
theory is the intensity of each concern at a particular point in time. In practice, everyone involved
with an innovation has all of these concerns all the
time, but to widely varying and changing degrees.
Practically speaking, it follows that whatever
concerns are most intense for a given individual at
a given time are those that warrant the most attention. In any case, the meaning of these concepts
should become more clear as we examine the respective stages one by one.

When the innovation is not a part of an individual's life, is not touching them in any way,
concerns are said to be at zero. There is little or
no awareness of the innovation, and it does not
represent a significant concern for that person.
This corresponds to Fuller's unrelated concerns.
But as soon as the innovation becomes imminent,
Stage One informational concerns arise. 'What is
it?' is the first thing people usually want to know
and, as a result, they may show an unprecedented
interest in learning more about the innovation. At
the same time, the recognition that it is now a
concrete part of the person's life produces intense
Stage Two personal concerns. 'What does this
innovation mean for me?' and 'How will using it
affect me?' are the almost inevitable expressions of
this intense personal response to new demands and
expectations. Both informational and personal
concerns would correspond to Fuller's rubric 'self
concerns'. All human beings, when confronted with a
new set of demands, experience some increase in
anxiety levels. This is particularly true when the
demands are linked with their means of livelihood,
which is already a high potential source of stress
for most people. Thus, when an innovation is

Figure 4.1:   Typical Expressions of Concern about the
              Innovation

	Stages of Concern	Expressions of Concern
	6 Refocusing	I have some ideas about something that would work even better.
I M P A C T	5 Collaboration	I am concerned about relating what I am doing with what other instructors are doing.
	4 Consequence	How is my use affecting students?
T A S K	3 Management	I seem to be spending all my time getting material ready.
S E L F	2 Personal	How will using it affect me?
	1 Informational	I would like to know more about it.
	0 Awareness	I am not concerned about it (the innovation).

introduced into a school, the affected teachers must not only master its techniques and procedures but also cope with the exacerbated stress it triggers, which only makes the mastering and assimilating that much harder.

As the person begins actually using the innovation, confronting the practical problems it inevitably entails, there is an increase in Stage Three management concerns: the questions now are on time, logistics, paperwork and organisation. These correspond to what Fuller labelled task concerns. One of the most common problems afflicting school improvement efforts has been the consistent failure to recognise the existence and significance of this stage. During this period, then, teachers are typically frantic and frustrated; their connection with the innovation may be tenuous, and their use of it superficial, since most of their time and energy are taken up with basic material and logistical preparations. It must also be clearly understood that this is not a transitory phenomenon: intense management concerns can be expected to last for a considerable length of time, one to two years or more, whenever an individual is introduced to something new.

If things go well enough, if enough time is allowed, if the requisite logistical support is provided and if the appropriate interventions are made by change facilitators, then hopefully the informational, personal and management concerns will reduce (Hall & Loucks, 1978). But this will not happen automatically or by accident. And even if it does, there is no guarantee that the diminishing of these concerns will result in individuals progressing to successive stages. Too often, the reduction of management concerns simply leads to the affected persons heaving a huge sigh of relief and then proceeding to 'coast' with the innovation, instead of developing interest in refining and hence perfecting their use of it. Undoubtedly, the temptation for teachers to coast is great, for there is never any shortage of subsequent problems and pressures building up to take its place. Another common tendency is for people to get so overwhelmed with their management concerns that they modify an innovation as much as possible in order to make themselves more comfortable with it. Unfortunately, this can easily lead to diluting the innovation out of existence, or simply abandoning it outright.

To a certain extent, these problems may be inevitable; but they have been aggravated in many instances by certain regrettable tendencies on the part of management. For one thing, we have traditionally done a poor job of monitoring innovations in progress with an eye toward diagnosing what is going on with them and, therefore, what needs to be done next. Thus, bereft of assistance and left to their own devices, teachers were perhaps inadvertently encouraged to engage in retrograde behaviour, provided that they did not disturb the appearance of things. At the same time, such evaluation or assessment as was undertaken by heads or LEAs was too often misdirected and ill-timed. In the past, evaluations have focused largely on the innovation's 'success' or 'failure', rather than on the needs and difficulties of those using or attempting to use it. In addition, summative evaluations have frequently been made within a year of adoption and initiation, in other words, precisely when teachers are immersed in intensive management concerns. As we have seen, the most common result of such well intentioned but poorly coordinated evaluation is a premature rejection of what might have been a promising innovation.

Thus, there is no guarantee that individuals using an innovation will ever progress beyond management concerns. If and when they do, however, there are three further stages they may pass through, all of which correspond to Fuller's impact concerns. In other words, having become sufficiently comfortable, and therefore self-confident with the innovation, they may now begin to direct more of their energy outward, toward the intended beneficiaries of the change: their students. SoC 4 consequence concerns focus on what effect teachers' actions have on students: is my use of this innovation helping my students and, if so, how? what adjustment could be made to increase student benefit? Any good teacher would of course be concerned about this from the outset, but that concern would initially be more or less smothered by the early, more intense, insistent personal needs. SoC 5 collaboration concerns express a desire to share ideas and work with other teachers using the same innovation. Collaboration means pooling energies and resources in an attempt mutually to discover ways to improve student outcomes. For many people this step, which might have seemed unduly threatening when they were first introduced to the innovation, may become increasingly appealing once they have achieved a basic level of competence with it and thus feel strong or confident. Finally, SoC 6 refocusing concerns involve the person's looking beyond the innovation toward something even better. In other words, 'What can I do that will really take my students further still?' This creative, inspirational approach, which stresses continual improvement, is the hallmark of the very best in teaching, as in any other field.

These, then, are the seven Stages of Concern. But the reader must always keep in mind that these categories are not graven in stone, any more than the various models and theoretical systems we have considered in previous chapters. Undoubtedly, a more streamlined model such as Fuller's might be used to convey the basic concept or, conversely, additional stages might be elaborated. Again, the order might be altered since, as we have tried to stress throughout, change is never the straightforward, linear process that charts and models make it out to be. The early stages, to be sure, would almost necessarily follow the progression we have outlined, since they plot the course from total ignorance through first acquaintance to beginning daily use of an innovation. But beyond SoC 3, as we have said, there may be no further progression at all; and if there is, it is likely to be far less predictable and rigid, depending almost entirely on each individual's orientation, viewpoint and degree of self-confidence. One person might go straight from management to consequence concerns; another might jump from management to collaboration and stay there. Beyond management concerns, then, the stages are decidedly nonhierarchical and, in some sense, optional. In any case, what SoC represents are certain common, predictable reactions to change that many people share; and in this lies its almost unlimited potential utility to heads and other change facilitators. Taken together and appropriately applied, these seven stages can be used to diagnose each affected individual and, therefore, the group as a whole, in connection with a given innovation. What are their feelings, reactions and attitudes toward the innovation? Where are they with respect to it, in their minds, hearts and classrooms? With this information, change facilitators can be better prepared to meet the challenges of innovation.

Using SoC. Now that we have the seven categories, the practitioner's obvious question is what do we do with them? Is this merely another neat theoretical formulation or does it have some immediate, practical use? In fact, as we shall see, SoC can be meaningfully applied to a wide range of real-life situations in schools and other institutions facing change. All these applications, however, are based on assessments of the relative strength of the various concerns held by different individuals and, thus, for the school as a whole.

There are three ways to collect information about an individual's concerns, which can then form the basis for making the assessments. One is the open-ended statement, in which the person is asked to write two or three sentences summarising their concerns about a particular innovation (Newlove & Hall, 1976). Subjects are to write in complete sentences and to be as open and frank as possible, rather than parroting what others have said. The facilitator can then code those statements, according to the stages of concern they represent. One advantage of the open-ended statement is that it yields not only strong SoC indicators but also data for content analysis. In other words, the individual's specific concerns, such as time, paperwork, or logistics, can be identified, as well as the generic concerns that SoC represents.

Another related possibility for information gathering is what is called a one-legged interview, so called, not because the participants stand on one leg, but because it is a brief, informal meeting frequently appearing to be spontaneous. This is similar in tone to the open-ended statement, except that it is conducted orally, informally and face-to-face (Hord & Loucks, 1980). Because it is so casual and short, it can more easily be fitted into practitioners' busy schedules, between classes, in the common room, or even during an unexpected encounter in the corridors. It is dependent on the interviewer's skills in eliciting and evaluating information. For this reason inspectors, heads and other change facilitators need to be trained in the art of asking appropriate 'starter' questions and of analysing the responses, in order to increase their effectiveness. One-legged interviews usually start in an extremely open fashion, with questions such as 'Are you aware of the new programme?' 'Are you using it?' or even 'Are you having any problems with it?' though this might lead the person being interviewed to focus exclusively on problems. Interviewers then try to keep their subjects talking long enough to gain a sense of their concerns and mentally code them. A skilled SoC interviewer can frequently accomplish this by sitting in the common room and listening to what is being said.

The most formal of the three information-gathering techniques is <u>The SoC Questionnaire</u> (SoCQ), a rigorous, psychometrically validated thirty-five-item instrument (Hall, George & Rutherford, 1979). It has been abundantly tested using an extensive data base, and can thus be employed with great confidence to identify indivi-duals' most intense concerns about a given innova-tion at a particular point in time. The validity of USA norms appears to hold up very well for other cultures, using the English language version; a decade of experience in six to seven countries, with the strongest evidence from widespread usage in Australia and Canada, has precipitated no need to make changes. If there is a language translation of the questionnaire, then it is advisable to check for the necessity of renorming. Utilisation of the English version SoCQ appears to produce no significant difference in norms in other countries despite cultural differences.

The SoCQ employs a seven-point Likert scale by means of which respondents can indicate their degree of agreement or disagreement with each of the thirty-five statements. The questionnaire thus automatically provides hard data, though unlike the open-ended statement, no content-related information is obtained. Data from the questionnaire may then be plotted on a graph as an aid to comparison and interpretation. Figure 4.2 depicts some typically resulting profiles corresponding to change in the user over time. Nonusers of an innovation are high in intensity on Stages 0, 1 and 2. New and inex-perienced users show a sharp elevation of management concerns. Experienced users (ie those with two or more years of innovation use) are more likely to have reduced informational, personal and management concerns; and, if the appropriate support and facilitative interventions have been taken, conse-quence and collaboration concerns may start to predominate. Finally, refocusing users, by virtue of experience, show very low Stage 0-2 concerns, low management concerns, and intense Stage 6 concerns. Intense refocusing concerns are the domain of only about six per cent of the data base population; these are the restless ones, the 'better mousetrap builders', who are always in search of ways to make improvements.

Stages of Concern, then, can tell us a number of important things about the status of an

Figure 4.2: Hypothesised Development of Stages of Concern

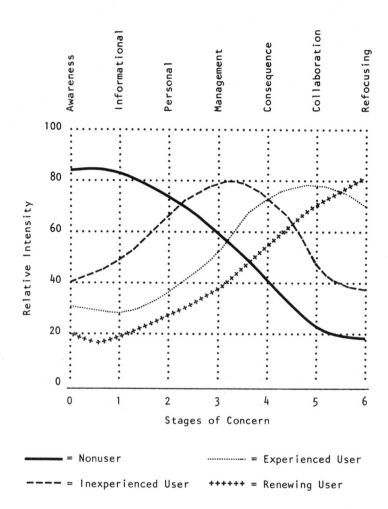

innovation-in-progress. First, it gives readings on the attitudinal status of individuals and clues about how to assist them. This can be helpful in assessing potential needs and problems before beginning initiation and during implementation. Based on these readings, SoC can be used to group individuals for the purpose of comparisons; it can also be an effective means of comparing results in different schools. Equally importantly, SoC can indicate for us a productive time to evaluate how well an innovation is working for students. This would not be when management concerns still predominate, since at this point implementation has not yet fully taken place. Rather, a better time would be when management concerns are reduced, showing that the individual is no longer consumed with the organisational and logistical aspects of the innovation. On this basis alone, SoC could have saved heads and LEAs a lot of wasted time and energy and doubtless rescued many prematurely scuttled innovations.

Obviously, different situations will demand different applications of SoC. One reason for the different information-gathering techniques is, in fact, to increase the whole component's flexibility. The SoCQ, because of its more rigorous nature, is used primarily for research and evaluation studies of teacher change and curriculum implementation. One part of an evaluation of a change might be to examine teachers' concerns to see if, indeed, their management concerns are reduced; if not, then more implementation and facilitation activities are clearly needed. Although the questionnaire might be considered too formal a procedure for certain situations in certain schools, it has been successfully applied in this way by some school leaders. Administered several times over the course of an innovation effort, it provides useful comparative data; in fact, the questionnaire has deliberately been limited to a single format in order to facilitate this function. In this context, the SoCQ would initially be administered early in a research study in order to collect base-line data, and periodically as a follow-up device, particularly after a significant intervention, in order to assess its effect. The questionnaire should probably not be used more than two or three times during a single school year, however, or it might begin to seem too tedious to staff.

The open-ended statement, by contrast, is popular with staff developers and facilitators in schools, especially when preparing to conduct inservice training, because the specific data it provides enables them to tailor that particular kind of intervention to their audience's needs. Like the SoCQ, however, it is not something that can be used too often without beginning to dilute its effectiveness. One-legged conferences, on the other hand, are a potentially effective means of follow-up that can be easily slipped into the working day. Far from alienating teachers, they can, if properly conducted, be perceived as signs of sympathetic interest and support; or, if the occasion warrants, they can be carried out in such a manner as to render them almost 'invisible' interventions. For this reason these informal, one-to-one exchanges may be repeated as often as seems desirable or necessary.

Ultimately, of course, it will be up to the head or other change facilitator to determine which method or, more probably, which mix of methods, proves most suited to the needs of the school. Within a broad framework, the individual facilitator enjoys considerable leeway to tailor the use of concerns to the particular objectives sought and the specific context in which it is employed. The importance of this facilitator, then, cannot be overstated. Without some recognised person to monitor and try actively to understand the complex process of change while it is occurring, the prospects for successful innovation will be gravely reduced. But even an informed and sympathetic facilitator, in order to be effective, will need to understand how SoC fits together with the other pieces of the model. For it is in combination that they can provide a complete, multidimensional picture of the ongoing process of change.

Levels of Use

To move from Stages of Concern to Levels of Use (LoU) is to undergo a major change in emphasis. SoC represents the affective dimension of change; that is, how it is perceived by individuals. LoU, on the other hand, focuses on people's behaviours and skills with respect to an innovation. In practice concerns and behaviours seem closely related and may even be inseparable; but for purposes of analysis, the distinction may help facilitate a more complete understanding of both dimensions and their interactive effects.

For LoU, then, the key question would be, 'How is the individual using the innovation?' To answer that question, a series of eight characterisations has been developed (Hall, Loucks, Rutherford & New-love, 1975). As with SoC, the individual is the focus of attention; based on their behaviour with respect to an innovation, people are said to be at one or another level of use (Figure 4.3). The most basic distinction is that between users and nonusers.

<u>Nonusers</u>. LoU recognises three different kinds of nonusers. When there is no behaviour whatsoever with the innovation, the person is said to be at LoU 0, <u>nonuse</u>. The new programme simply has no place in the person's life, and no action is being taken with respect to it. As soon as the person begins showing interest in the innovation, however, and exhibiting the behaviours of looking for information about it, he or she is at LoU I, <u>orientation</u>. This behaviour may take any number of forms: attending a workshop to learn about the innovation, discussing it with colleagues, visiting another school that is already using it, reading about it or receiving a visit from a publisher's representative. The important point is that some interaction between an innovation and its potential user is taking place on an informational level.

LoU II, <u>preparation</u>, has been reached when the person indicates an intention to use the innovation, a concrete decision has been made and a specified time has been set to begin. Typical behaviours at this level would include stocking the shelves, ordering books and materials and getting equipment ready--all practical actions directly related to actual use of the innovation. Both levels I and II presuppose some degree of involvement with the innovation and, in level II, a decision to pursue or permit that involvement. This may be made by the individual or, in some instances, it will have been made for them by a coordinator or superior. For our present purposes, however, no distinction is drawn between these two situations, since we are focusing only on behaviour here. As long as the person consents to the decision, he or she is said to be at LoU II.

If these distinctions seem a little artificial, they are made for good reason. In the first place, they did not originate as theoretical constructs; rather, these three types of nonusers were discov-

Figure 4.3: Levels of Use Typical Behaviours

Level of Use	Behavioural Indices of Level
VI Renewal	The user is seeking more effective alternatives to the established use of the innovation.
V Integration	The user is making deliberate efforts to coordinate with others in using the innovation.
IVB Refinement	The user is making changes to increase outcomes.
IVA Routine	The user is making few or no changes and has an established pattern of use.
III Mechanical Use	The user is making changes to organise better use of the innovation.
II Preparation	The individual is preparing to use the innovation.
I Orientation	The individual is seeking information about the innovation.
0 Nonuse	No action is being taken with respect to the innovation.

U
S
E
R

N
O
N
U
S
E
R

111

ered in our fieldwork in schools and other institutions and we have therefore tried to develop a model that describes that reality. Second, and equally important for the change facilitator (CF), the appropriate types of facilitative interventions will be very different for each level of nonuse. Take, for example, a CF responsible for introducing computer studies into a school. If the staff are at LoU 0, the facilitator's task is to provide interventions that will pique their interest in exploring the innovation and so advancing to LoU I. If, on the other hand, people are already at LoU I, the facilitator will want to focus on providing them with sufficient information, and making a persuasive enough case, to encourage them to move to LoU II. And in the case of LoU II people, the appropriate interventions would be those that will help them to prepare for actually using the innovation. Thus, instead of providing them with information <u>about</u> it, they should be getting training, logistical support and information oriented toward implementing and managing its use in their classrooms.

<u>Users</u>. At this point, then, we cross the line dividing nonuse from use, which is perhaps the most fundamental distinction one can make with respect to an innovation. This does not mean, however, that our facilitation is over, nor that the innovation can be said to be fully implemented. In fact, implementation is just beginning; LoU distinguishes five types of users whose behaviours collectively outline the territory still to be covered.

Everyone beginning to use an innovation, at least as we have defined it, starts at LoU III, <u>mechanical use</u>. At this level, the person is inexperienced and is still experimenting with the innovation, trying to make it work. Typically, the Level III person is preoccupied with organisational and logistical considerations, such as getting organised, locating materials, making plans and timetables and setting up the classroom. The combined demands of mastering the new programme, introducing it to students and still maintaining order tend to absorb a great deal of time and energy, which contributes to a generally poorly coordinated and limited use of the innovation. At this point, the person simply lacks the experience and the practical and emotional resources to look much beyond the next day's preparations. The principal interest of Level III users is in seeking out

ways to make use of the innovation easier for them;
any experimentation or modification of the programme
that might be undertaken would be strictly
user-oriented. People usually stay at Level III for
a long time; indeed, they well may never get beyond
it unless they receive sufficient training in how to
use the innovation, one-to-one coaching by a change
facilitator to help them resolve specific problems,
and adequate logistical support. In any case, these
interventions can only reduce the amount of time
spent at Level III, by enabling the user to gain
experience more quickly; they cannot, however,
eliminate this necessary and inevitable step.

Given sufficient time to learn about and use
the innovation, and adequate interventions to
support that use, it eventually becomes stabilised.
At this point, we say that the person has reached
LoU IVA, routine. The immediate practical dilemmas
have been resolved and a comfortable plateau has
been reached. Rather than seeking to make changes,
the Level IVA user is more likely to be breathing a
sigh of relief. The problems and stresses that
inevitably accompany innovation have been survived
and the person's reaction is likely to be, 'Why mess
with a good thing?' It should be noted here that
there is nothing wrong with LoU IVA, nor does it
necessarily imply an acceptable but poor quality
level of use. On the contrary, it may be a richly
elaborated, very effective pattern of innovation
use; but it is stabilised. This stability, coming
on the heels of a period of change and stress,
fulfils a crucial function for most people. Regardless of what they do subsequently, almost everyone
will need some period of IVA use before they will be
ready to move onward.

Beyond IVA, the user's relationship with the
innovation changes yet again. Instead of struggling
merely to survive with it, or being content to
adhere to an established pattern of its use, at the
highest three levels the person begins actively
seeking ways to change it that will improve student
outcomes. The first of these is Level IVB, refinement, in which changes may be targeted at a particular subgroup of students, fast or slow learners, for
instance, or at the group as a whole. The changes
may affect the programme itself or the way it is
delivered, used or managed. The key fact is that
the user's activity is now outwardly directed;
instead of making changes to help themselves use the
programme, Level IVB people are experimenting with
ways to help students use it more fruitfully.

Furthermore, these changes are not, as is often the case with the more desperate experiments of Level III users, mere shots in the dark; rather, they are based on a viable level of understanding of the innovation and imply some assessment, whether formal or informal, of its problems and potential.

Thus far, our attention has been focused exclusively on individuals acting independently of one another, within their separate classrooms or other spheres of action. But this is not the only medium for innovation use. When two or more people are collaborating on a programme or project, pooling their ideas and energies and resources to produce better results for their students or other clients, they are at LoU V, integration. This is essentially the same as LoU IVB, except that it is now a cooperative venture. It could take the form of teaching as a team or some less visible means of mutual support. It is not integration if the collaboration is primarily user-oriented: for example, when two users propose to work together simply in order to reduce their own workloads. Thus, although LoU looks chiefly at a person's behaviour, some consideration of their motives with respect to the innovation may also be necessary, at least in certain cases.

Finally, the most restlessly creative individuals, those who never cease to seek ways to make further improvements, may eventually reach LoU VI, renewal. At this point, it could almost be said that the original innovation has already been outgrown. The Level VI person, having seen or sensed the inherent limits in the established pattern of innovation use, now prepares to move beyond them, either by making some major fundamental alteration of it or by introducing a cluster of smaller changes that collectively accomplish the same end. Thus, in a sense, the particular innovation is completed, not by abandonment or rigid stratification, but by remerging it with the ongoing innovation stream.

Information gathering. There are two procedures for collecting LoU information. As with SoC, the different methods correspond to the varying needs of different groups of people. Unlike SoC, however, there is no written instrument that can successfully elicit the necessary information for LoU. Many people have experimented with this, but it simply has not worked, apparently because no written format has been found that is open enough to take sufficient account of individuals' variant responses. For this reason, we have concluded that LoU data acquisition requires a one-to-one interview.

The first kind of interview uses what is called the branching technique; its primary purpose is to help change facilitators and other practitioners obtain a broad, global sense of an individual's level of use of an innovation as a prerequisite to offering the person appropriate assistance. The branching technique is used in the context of a one-legged interview, which, as described in the section of Stages of Concern, is a brief, informal 'conversation'. It starts with the basic question, 'Are you using the innovation?' and, based on the answer, directs the interview along either the user or nonuser branch. In the case of a 'no' response, the nonuser branch is followed. It contains questions that will identify the individual at either LoU 0, I or II: 'Have you decided to use the innovation and have set a date to begin?' A 'yes' answer establishes LoU II. If the response is 'no', then the question, 'Are you currently looking for information about the innovation?' is used. A 'yes' response indicates LoU I; a 'no' response suggests LoU 0.

Similarly, by following through the appropriate series of user questions, the interviewer gains a general idea of the individual's overall level of use: If a 'no' response is gained from the first question, 'Are you making changes in your use of the innovation?', then LoU IVA is likely. If this question is answered with a 'yes', then 'What kinds of changes are you making?' is in order. If the response contains user-oriented changes, then LoU III is suggested; if the response is impact-oriented, then further questions are required to sort out LoU IVB, V, or VI: 'Are you coordinating your use of the innovation with other users?' A 'no' response suggests LoU IVB or VI; a 'yes' response is a clue to LoU V or VI. If an additional question, 'Are you planning or exploring major modifications, or replacing the innovation?' elicits 'yes', then LoU VI is established. Further explication and/or training would prepare the facilitator for using this technique to acquire soft data on which to base assistance and support for the individual.

For certain applications, however, more detailed information is required. Educational researchers and evaluators, in particular, need hard data in connection with research studies and other more formal analyses. For this purpose, they must first undergo an extensive three-day training programme in the course of which they learn the entire LoU system: interviewing protocol, LoU categories and how to rate the data collected. Having mastered these procedures, the interviewer can then construct a matrix from the data that reveals more in-depth information about an individual's patterns of use. The key to this enhanced detail is the employment, in addition to the <u>levels</u> of use, of seven <u>categories</u>.

Briefly stated, these seven categories represent additional ways of describing an individual's behaviour with respect to an innovation. Only one of them, Performing, refers to the teacher's classroom activity as the innovation is operationalised; the remaining six focus on other aspects of the relationship between innovation and user. The first category, Knowledge, concerns the subject's theoretical and practical understanding of the innovation, which is the basis for all subsequent interaction. This is cognitive knowledge related to the characteristics of the innovation, how to use it and consequences of its use. The next four categories describe various behaviours toward or with the innovation: Acquiring Information, Sharing, Assessing and Planning. Acquiring Information involves the solicitation of information about the innovation through questioning resource people, corresponding with agencies, reviewing printed materials or making visits. Discussion of the innovation with others is the focus of Sharing: plans, ideas, resources, outcomes and problems related to innovation use. In Assessing, the potential or actual use of the innovation or some aspect of it is examined mentally or through collection and analysis of data. Included in Planning are such activities as designing and outlining short and long range steps to be taken during innovation adoption and implementation, ie align resources, develop timetables, meet with others to organise. The last category, Status Reporting, considers the subject's perceptions of their use of the innovation.

Within the context of the LoU interview, then, these seven categories constitute another tool for placing an individual's behaviour at the appropriate level. The interview itself is a structured but not locked-in format; using it, the skilled LoU interviewer can uncover a great deal about a person's current status with an innovation. The most important point to remember here is that the same person may be at different levels in different categories. Overall, for example, the subject may be at Level IVA, routine, but be <u>planning</u> at Level IVB, refinement. By assessing the subject's behaviour in each category and forming a composite picture, a more detailed and accurate representation of the person's total working relationship with the innovation can be achieved.

<u>Implications of LoU</u>. Those readers who feel overwhelmed by this proliferation of categories and criteria, or for whom it appears too removed from the daily realities of schools, may take comfort in the knowledge that some simplification is possible. Essentially, the five user levels can be characterised on the basis of a single factor: changes. The Level III person makes experimental changes in an effort to master using the innovation; at Level IVA, a routine has been established and there is no change whatsoever. Beyond this point, changes are being made primarily to benefit clients: either by the user alone (IVB), in conjunction with other users (V), or in such a way as to alter fundamentally the nature of the innovation (VI).

One common problem people have with LoU is distinguishing between Levels IVB, refinement, and VI, renewal. This is a matter of degree; specifically speaking, the difference between them is idiosyncratic to each innovation. Given sufficient understanding of the latter, the distinction should become apparent. In general terms, however, it may be likened to the different steps a dissatisfied television viewer might take, whether fine-tuning the picture (IVB), or simply changing the channel (VI).

Perhaps the most important thing to keep in mind when using LoU is that as with SoC, each level of use is <u>a snapshot in time</u>. That is, the picture it gives of an individual's innovation use is an immediate and current one, but subject to change. The progression from one level to another is neither automatic nor necessarily linear, or even monodirectional, though at the earlier levels it is more likely to be both of these. Beyond Level III, however, there is considerably greater room for variation. For example, a teacher may have made impact-related alterations in an innovation three months ago; but now, having stabilised those refinements and been satisfied with the results, the same person may not be making any further changes. Thus, although a movement from LoU IVB 'back' to LoU IVA has been described, it cannot in any sense be considered a regression.

Another strong temptation, after reviewing the 'Expressions' and 'Behaviours' charts, is rigidly to lock in the numbered Levels of Use with their respective Stages of Concern. Obviously, there is a strong connection between these two dimensions and, especially at the upper or lower stages or levels, the correspondence may be quite direct. But the essence of the entire CBAM model is <u>looking at each of these dimensions for an individual separately</u>; this means, among other things, allowing for the full scope of human variation. Particularly in the later stages, a wide range of possible patterns exists for both SoC and LoU, which will therefore intersect in a variety of ways, according to each individual's specific problems, needs and interests. To gain a complete and accurate understanding of the current reality of a specific change within a given context, full account must be taken of both of these dimensions, as well as Innovation Configurations (IC), to which we now turn.

Innovation Configurations
The concept of Innovation Configurations entails another major shift in emphasis. Both SoC and LoU are primarily concerned with the user of an innovation--whether in terms of the person's feelings about it or behaviour with respect to it. In either case, the <u>person</u> is the centre of attention, and the innovation is, in a sense, peripheral. The obvious problem with such distinctions lies in attempting to separate the innovation as an objective entity or fact from people's feelings about it; but that is done in the CBAM model through the use of Innovation Configurations. In IC, the <u>innovation itself</u> is the focus of attention, and the person's behaviour, though critical, is seen chiefly as a means of gauging <u>exactly what the innovation is</u> in the context of that person's use of it.

This change in emphasis came about as a result of our experiences in the field. When we visited schools and talked to teachers about a particular innovation, asking them if they were using it, many said they were. When we asked them to describe what they were doing, we soon discovered that, in many instances, the 'it' they were using bore little resemblance to the 'it' described by their colleague across the corridor and perhaps even less to the innovation's original conception. The fact is that no two teachers, whether within the same building or across schools, use an innovation in precisely the same way. Rather, different teachers will incorporate into their practice different portions of the new programme, used in conjunction, in most cases, with some percentage of whatever they were doing before—which will also show considerable variation. Thus, both the content and extent of new programme use will vary tremendously, even among individuals within the same institution. And for researchers, change facilitators and others with a need to evaluate innovation use, this means that not only the 'how' but also the 'what' of innovation use must be taken into consideration. It simply is not possible to assume that we know what an innovation looks like in practice in a given classroom, however well versed we may be in its theoretical form and appearance. Hence the vital importance of IC, both in its own right and as a means of explaining SoC and LoU.

Using Innovation Configurations. The application of the innovation configurations procedure to a given innovation entails a number of steps in the development of an innovation configuration checklist (see Figure 4.4). The key to the entire process is to consider the innovation in terms of its parts or components. These are the building blocks from which the innovation is built; they will naturally be different for each innovation. In addition, potential variations of each component need to be considered. Thus, in order to determine the components of a given innovation, it is generally necessary to interview both developers and facilitators. Previous experience has shown the following three questions to be most useful: what would you observe when the innovation is operational? what would teachers and others be doing? and what are the critical components of the innovation? (Hall & Loucks, 1981). Based on the responses to these questions, a preliminary list of components and their variations can be assembled, to be refined and improved in the course of additional checklist development. A further distinction is drawn between essential and related components; that is, between those that must be present and those that may optionally be used to enhance innovation use.

Figure 4.4: A Procedure for Identifying Innovation
Configurations

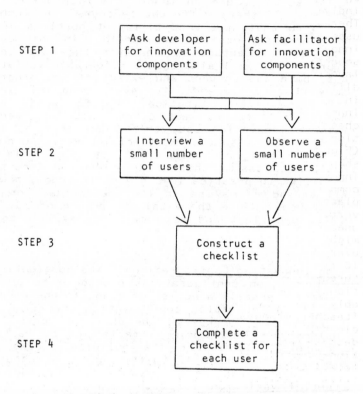

Once an innovation's components and variations have been specified, the next step is to construct an appropriate checklist by means of which each individual's use of the innovation can be assessed. There are various types of checklists that may be used, depending on both the nature of the particular innovation in question and the specific information sought. One common type might be likened to a laundry list (see Figure 4.5): that is, it lists different variations for each component, resulting in a general characterisation of the individual's innovation use. This is the most basic kind of checklist; it provides a limited amount of information. A part of a more complex checklist format (Figure 4.6) gives some indication of the relationship between the individual's practice and the innovation's preferred form. In this format, the components and their respective variations are placed on a least-to-most-desirable continuum, with vertical lines to delineate ideal, acceptable and unacceptable behaviour. Other kinds of checklists might suggest themselves in the context of a particular innovation. The most important feature of any IC checklist, however, is that it should be <u>struc-tured in operational terms</u>: that is, the descriptions of behaviour should employ verbs, and preferably subjects also, such as 'teacher uses x' or 'teacher manages x', in order to make it eminently clear <u>who is doing what</u>. In this sense, then, and despite what we said earlier about its being innovation-centred, IC is also, like LoU, fundamentally behavioural. If this seems confusing, it may be taken as merely an additional illustration of the plain impossibility of drawing clear and immutable distinctions between an innovation and its actual use.

The sum total, then, of all of an individual's specific responses to the various items on a checklist comprises an <u>innovation configuration</u>. It represents the unique <u>operational form</u> of the innovation employed by that person, consisting of the identified components or variants combined in a particular way. It should be noted here that, generally speaking, the particular grouping or sequence of components is not important, though with respect to a given innovation it may be; in this as in other aspects, everything depends on the specific nature of the innovation in question. For the most part, however, grouping or sequence will not matter, as long as all the essential components are present and accounted for.

Figure 4.5: Mathematics Programme Checklist

Please check one choice for each of the six categories below
that is the most descriptive of your mathematics instruction.

1. Instructional materials:
   _____ (1) Uses primarily textbook(s)
   _____ (2) Uses primarily material packs provided by the
             programme
   _____ (3) Uses wide variety of materials: possibly
             including text(s); programme packs; games; kits;
             pebbles, buttons, counters or other objects for
             concept development

2. Grouping:
   _____ (1) Teaches whole class or two groups
   _____ (2) Teaches three or more groups
   _____ (3) Teaches individuals only, no grouping

3. Objectives:
   _____ (1) Programme objectives are taught largely in
             sequence
   _____ (2) Programme objectives are taught largely out of
             sequence
   _____ (3) Programme objectives are not taught

4. Testing:
   _____ (1) Tests are given for each objective
   _____ (2) Tests are given for groups of objectives
   _____ (3) No tests are given

5. Test Results:
   _____ (1) Test results determine next steps of individual
             students
   _____ (2) If most of group passes test, the group goes on
             and those who failed are given special help
   _____ (3) If most of group passes test, the group goes on
             and no special help is given those who fail

6. Record-Keeping:
   _____ (1) Records are kept by objective for each child
   _____ (2) Records are kept other than by objective for each
             child
   _____ (3) No records are kept

Figure 4.6: More Complex Checklist

1. Materials and Equipment		
At least 5 different programme materials are used with each child each session.	At least 3 different programme materials are used with each child each session.	Fewer than 3 different programme materials are used with each child each session.
2. Diagnosis		
Children are diagnosed individually using a combination of tests and teacher judgement.	Children are diagnosed individually using teacher judgement only.	Children are not diagnosed individually.
3. Record-Keeping		
Individual Record Sheets are used to record diagnosis and prescription.	No Individual Record Sheets are used.	
4. Use of Teaching Technique		
Continually re-adjusts task according to child's needs; uses rewards to reinforce student success.	Does not continually re-adjust task according to child's needs; does not use rewards.	
5. Grouping		
Children are taught in pairs.	Children are not taught in pairs.	
6. Timetabling		
Children are taught for 30 min. 3 times per week. Each session is equally divided between children.	Children are taught for 30 min. 3 times per week, time for each child and each task varies slightly when necessary.	Children not taught for 30 min. 3 times per week, or time for each child and each task varies markedly or is not considered.

CODE: ——— Variations to the right are unacceptable; variations to the left are acceptable.

— — Variations to the left are ideal, as prescribed by the developer.

The distinctions between ideal, acceptable and unacceptable behaviour indicated in our second checklist format (Figure 4.6) are not meant to be restrictive, as they might at first seem. Though they would appear to suggest a bias toward a particular means of using an innovation, we are not promoting the concept of fidelity, per se. The real objectives of such an IC checklist are, rather, to help users and facilitators understand what a given programme is, how it might be put into practice and which of these possible practices seem to promise the best kinds of outcomes for students and/or teachers.

IC Implications and Applications. Innovations rarely come about in a vacuum. Rather, the evolution of ideas and practices is generally a cooperative venture in which input and inspiration from a great many people and places come together synergistically to yield more fruitful results. Certainly, the concept of innovation configurations did not spring fully formed like Aphrodite from the head of Zeus. As we saw in Chapter One of this volume, the Rand Study (Berman & McLaughlin, 1975) assessed different patterns of innovation use, distinguishing three basic types, nonimplementation and cooptation and mutual adaptation, and citing the latter as not only a desirable but indeed an essential prerequisite to successful implementation of change. According to this approach, both the innovation and the local setting have to be adjusted to each other, in order to produce a change that is in keeping with the spirit of the programme and appropriate to the local context.

The concept of innovation configuration is essential to a full appreciation of mutual adaptation. As we have indicated, individual variation in innovation use is inevitable; IC can be an invaluable tool both in assessing what sort of adaptation has already taken place and in assuring that it falls within acceptable limits in terms of the desired results. Rather than viewing individual variations in practice as unfortunate but unavoidable aberrations, moreover, this perspective promotes a more optimistic view of them as potential means of releasing each teacher's creativity—which is ultimately the most effective educational innovation of all.

Beyond this, the concept of innovation configurations offers many things to many people, and something to almost everyone connected with educational innovation. At every stage of the innovation process, IC can be fruitfully used. Even before initiation begins, this innovation-based dimension has several relevant applications. For example, 'The first rule of intelligent tinkering is <u>save all the pieces</u>' and the IC checklist is a way to do precisely that. Thus, before introducing change, the checklist can be used to assess a teacher's prior practice, to identify what is already in place in order to avoid throwing the baby out with the bathwater in an innovative frenzy. The checklist can also be used to help pinpoint the expectations of developers and users alike by indicating, through its range of variant behaviours, some of the possible patterns of innovation use.

In addition, IC provides an excellent means of introducing a new programme to teachers or other prospective users. Virtually any programme can be analysed and broken into its component parts in order to facilitate talking about it. As experience has shown, it can be extremely useful to do so at the outset, as a way of helping teachers understand the innovation in operational, functional terms. Not surprisingly, IC has become very popular with practitioners, because of the clarity provided by this structured approach. Too often, innovations are presented to practitioners on a somewhat abstract basis, accompanied by a lot of talk about how good they are, about the philosophical assumptions on which they are based or the exalted goals they are expected to accomplish. Unfortunately, this kind of presentation ignores or overlooks precisely what teachers most want to know, that is, what will we be doing in the classroom? How will the innovation look in practice? How will it affect the current programme? Innovation configurations can provide concise, coherent answers to these and similar user-oriented questions, which explains why it has been so eagerly embraced by practitioners faced with the prospect of implementing innovations and naturally desiring to know what, precisely, they are.

Once an innovation has been introduced and implementation is under way, the innovation configuration checklist has obvious applicability. By zeroing in on exactly what is going on with the innovation within individual classrooms, IC helps practitioners understand what is happening in their schools during the challenging and often difficult course of the change process. For change facilitators, the IC checklist is another vital tool for analysing individuals' current behaviour with an innovation and placing it in an appropriate context, in order to identify each person's needs and determine suitable interventions to address them. Finally, innovation configurations represent an additional dimension for assessing change as it occurs in educational institutions and the individuals within them; as such, it can be extremely useful in the evaluation of the progress and status of an innovation. Thus, at every point along the change continuum, IC, in conjunction with the other dimensions of the CBAM model, offers insights and tools for the understanding and promotion of successful innovation.

Throughout this chapter, as we have outlined and discussed the various dimensions of CBAM and their applications to educational innovation, we have tried to stress both their inherently interlocking nature and the unequivocal need for direct, focused action in support of change. Repeated reference has been made to the change facilitator and the broad kinds of actions this person or persons might take. But we have not yet spelled out in sufficient detail what the change facilitator does, and how this person's theoretical or actual behaviour fits into the overall picture of the change process we have been gradually assembling.

Even the most skilled craftsperson cannot work without the appropriate tools, and we have accordingly devoted our attention and effort to describing and illustrating a particular set of tools for promoting and for gauging change in schools. Having done so, however, it is now time to move on to a more comprehensive perspective on their use; that is, to move from these diagnostic dimensions of change to what is essentially a prescriptive dimension. In the next chapter, then, I introduce and discuss Interventions, the prescriptive dimension of CBAM which subsumes and orchestrates the contributions of the previous three. Here the reader will find both clarification of the roles and functions of change facilitators and explication of the ways in which the different dimensions of CBAM interlock and interact within the context of a particular innovation effort.

REFERENCES

Berman, P., & McLaughlin, M. W. (1975). Federal programs supporting educational change, Vol. IV: The findings in review. Santa Monica, CA: Rand Corporation.

Fuller, F. F. (1969). Concerns of teachers: A developmental conceptualisation. American Educational Research Journal, 6(2), 207-226.

Fuller, F.F. (1973). Teacher education and the psychology of behavior change: A conceptualization of the process of affective change of preservice teachers. Austin: Research and Development Center for Teacher Education, The University of Texas at Austin.

Gabriel, J. (1957). An analysis of the emotional problems of the teacher in the classroom. Melbourne, Australia: F.W. Cheshire.

Hall, G. E., George, A. A. & Rutherford, W. L. (1979). Measuring stages of concern about the innovation: A manual for use of the SoC questionnaire. Austin: Research and Development Center for Teacher Education, The University of Texas at Austin.

Hall, G. E. & Loucks, S. F. (1978). Teacher concerns as a basis for facilitating and personalising staff development. Teachers College Record, 80(1), 36-53.

Hall, G.E. & Loucks, S.F. (1981). Program definition and adaptation: Implications for inservice. Journal of Research and Development in Education, 14 (2), 46-58.

Hall, G. E., Loucks, S. F., Rutherford, W. L. &
Newlove, B. W. (1975). Levels of use of the
innovation: A framework for analyzing innovation adoption. The Journal of Teacher Education, 26(1), 52-56.

Hall, G. E. & Rutherford, W. L. (1976). Concerns of
teachers about implementing team teaching.
Educational Leadership, 34(3), 227-233.

Hall, G.E., Wallace, R.C., & Dossett, W.A. (1973).
A developmental conceptualization of the
adoption process within educational institu-
tions. Austin: Research and Development
Center for Teacher Education, The University of
Texas at Austin.

Hord, S. M. & Loucks, S. F. (1980). A concerns-
based model for the delivery of inservice.
Austin: Research and Development Center for
Teacher Education, The University of Texas at
Austin.

Newlove, B. W. & Hall, G. E. (1976). A manual for
assessing open-ended statements of concern
about an innovation. Austin: Research and
Development Center for Teacher Education, The
University of Texas at Austin.

Rogers, E.M., & Shoemaker, F.F. (1971). Communication of innovations: A cross cultural approach
(2nd ed.). New York: Free Press.

Chapter 5

PUTTING IT ALL TOGETHER

In the previous pages, I have introduced a set of
concepts whose application to a specific situation
or setting yields variables by means of which we can
evaluate and characterise the status of people and
programmes in the process of change. I have
described the concepts and the assessment procedure
or device that accompanies each one, and have also
attempted to give at least some indication of their
respective uses. Still, from a practical standpoint, the nagging question that remains is, 'So
what?' That is, given all these concepts and
measures, what can be done with them? Do they
really make a difference, and if so, does it justify
the requisite time and energy investment by busy
practitioners? To some extent, at least, these are
clearly questions that individuals will have to
answer for themselves, based on their personal
concerns and specific situations. But certainly a
closer look at some of the ways CBAM is used in
different settings and at different points along the
change continuum can help provide a basis for
informed decision making.

APPLICATIONS OF CBAM DIAGNOSTIC DIMENSIONS

The uses of the CBAM model, whether in its entirety
or in part, are as varied as the different innovations and contexts to which it is applied. Once the
real significance of the different dimensions and
their interrelations is understood, an ever greater
range and number of specific applications may
suggest themselves. Speaking broadly, however,
there are three general questions that the CBAM can
help answer: What would I like to see happen with
the innovation? How can I make that happen? and How

129

is it going? Each of these questions suggests a particular function or area of use, which may be appropriate to different stages in the innovation process, though in many cases, once again, their applicability transcends purely temporal considerations. The first of these, then, is goal setting.

Goal Setting

One of the most common causes of innovation failure in the past has been lack of adequate attention to goal setting. In the absence of clear cut, concisely elaborated goals, the confusion that inevitably accompanies any major change of practice tends to multiply, thereby compounding the difficulties already faced. In addition to the pressures to assimilate new skills, teachers must struggle to cope with their uncertainties concerning what is expected both of them and of the new programme itself. And for heads and other change facilitators the lack of explicit goals can be at least equally problematical, when they are trying to respond to the pressure to 'produce results' without being entirely certain themselves what the expected results are, what facilitative actions their attainment might require or how they might be recognised, once achieved.

At the same time, however, it must be acknowledged that, for busy practitioners, establishing meaningful goals is not an easy task. As we noted in the last chapter, innovations are often described by their developers in extremely broad, vague terms that may seem to have little relevance to the realities of classroom and school administration and thus give few clues as to what users may reasonably expect to accomplish. In addition, the time and resources needed to effect a comprehensive analysis, set specific goals and follow through with them are, too often, simply not available. Regrettably, a far more common pattern is for an innovation to be thrust upon the school with little warning, accompanied only by a two-day INSET programme in the autumn and demands for higher reading scores by June or July. Under such conditions, heads accustomed to crowded schedules and to operating in a perennial state of emergency may be inclined to view the idea of a leisurely, detached and lengthy period of analysis and preparation for action as Utopian, if not downright ludicrous.

Notwithstanding the restraints of time and resource allocation, however, goal setting, to differing degrees and at various levels, remains a viable and useful option. The flexibility and interlocking nature of the three diagnostic dimensions of CBAM allows for a variety of applications, depending on the scope and depth required; and it is not always necessary, or even desirable, to use all three dimensions in a given situation, particularly where limited, short-term objectives are concerned. This is not to say that SoC, LoU and IC do not all have important contributions to make to the goal-setting process: assuredly, they do; and ideally, their joint use in making an explicit statement of what should be happening in classrooms after the delivery of adequate INSET and other assistance is highly desirable. But realistically speaking, given the decidedly less-than-ideal conditions that all too often prevail in schools, this may not always be possible. The following examples, then, suggest concrete ways that one or more dimensions of CBAM may be applied to a variety of goal-setting situations, in order to help readers understand and visualise the practical uses of these vital tools.

Suppose, for example, that we want to implement a new vocational education programme. The programme shows great promise of enabling the maximum number of school leavers successfully to enter the job market. For this to happen, however, teachers must successfully use it first. Thus, we might decide at the outset that we will not be satisfied with our implementation effort until or unless we have determined that all teachers using the innovation have reached at least a routine level of use (LoU IVA), with relatively low self and task concerns, and a minimally acceptable innovation configuration, that is, one in which all essential components are in use. This is a somewhat moderate objective; a more ambitious one might be to state that every teacher should be at least at LoU IVB, refinement, with high impact concerns and an ideal innovation configuration; conversely, a preliminary expectation might prescribe that every teacher be at least at a mechanical level of use (LoU III), with Stage 3-6 concerns higher than Stages 0-2, and be using at least two-thirds of the programme's components. The specifics are, of course, highly variable and subject to the demands of the given situation, particularly time and resource considerations. But the point is that these are <u>objectively measurable goals</u> whose attainment can be unequivocally demonstrated, thus leaving little room for the kind of uncertainty and floundering around that may result from the more usual ambiguous verbal goal descriptions.

Now let us suppose, however, that we find ourselves in a less ideal, less comprehensive situation. If, for example, we are called upon to try to save a foundering programme, a realistic goal might be merely to reduce teachers' management or personal concerns, assuming that CBAM diagnosis had shown this to be part of the problem. Again, for a facilitator preparing for a two-hour awareness INSET session, the goal might be to increase informational concerns while minimising personal concerns. Or, in a one-day session on analysis of classroom interactions, the goal might be to increase the total number of teachers who are at the refinement level of use. Thus, goal setting may be effective in short-term as well as long-term applications, and with almost any number of dimensions employed, depending on what user change is required or desired.

In the case of long-term goals, the realisation of which may take several years, a somewhat different rationale is at work. Having a fixed objective against which to measure the relative motion of initiation and implementation efforts can assist both users and facilitators in keeping perspective on where they are and where they have been with the innovation. Establishing long-term goals can also aid in promoting eventual institutionalisation. As we saw in Chapter Two, even promising and apparently stable innovations not uncommonly seem to wither on the vine and die as soon as their special funding disappears. Lack of recognition of institutionalisation as a vital subprocess of educational change has undoubtedly contributed to this problem. Thus a detailed, coherent set of long-term goals, which provides an unambiguous picture of how both users and use are expected to look after sufficient implementation has been carried out, helps us know if and when institutionalisation has been achieved (Hord and Hall, 1986). Indeed, it could be said that institutionalisation means achieving your goals with an innovation.

Supporting Change

Once appropriate goals have been set and initiation begun, the facilitator's attention can begin to shift to designing and delivering INSET activities, classroom monitoring and other generally more active means of facilitating change. In this phase, the relevance of SoC, LoU and IC to the facilitator's daily work is perhaps more obvious. As we have shown in the previous chapter in our separate discussions of these three diagnostic dimensions of CBAM, each of them can be used to provide a distinct yet complementary perspective on the innovation as a living entity in the context of daily use. Taken together, they can give the head or other change facilitator the kind of detailed, multidimensional picture of what is happening within the school at a given point in time, and how that current behaviour relates to prior practice and to future goals. Such a picture is invaluable as a basis for designing and carrying out interventions that will maximise the innovation's chances for successful implementation and institutionalisation.

As with goal setting, the nuts-and-bolts field work of supporting change also admits a variety of short-term, long-term, full or partial CBAM applications. Here, too, a complex, comprehensive master plan extending over a period of several years and embracing every aspect of change and every kind of intervention might be characterised as the ideal approach; indeed, the CBAM does support this kind of in-depth planning and plotting of facilitator interventions. A more detailed look at the concept of interventions, its relationship with the three diagnostic dimensions and its applications within the CBAM model as a whole is given in a subsequent section of this chapter. But when time and resources are limited, less extensive, smaller scale applications are also possible and potentially useful.

Many of the specific applications of CBAM concepts to a change effort in progress are concerned with INSET, its appropriate design and management. Use of these dimensions, particularly Stages of Concern, can mean the difference between excessively general and theoretical staff development presentations with little practical impact and productive sessions, and focusing on real staff needs that contribute significantly to effective implementation. Some specific examples should help clarify the basic concept.

One of the most useful and broadly applicable CBAM tools is the open-ended concerns statement, which can easily be tailored to meet the needs of specific situations. For instance, when called upon to provide follow-up INSET in the first or second year of programme use, a head or other facilitator might ask teachers to complete such a statement in advance of the INSET session. Once the statements had been read through and scored, they could provide valuable insights into what specific areas or concerns might be most fruitfully addressed with that particular group at that specific time. The same approach could be used by an LEA adviser. For someone less familiar with the school and staff, it might be worthwhile to request concerns statements in two areas: one dealing with the particular programme and the other with the school, or with teaching, in general. Once again, the data so obtained could be a great help both in planning and in anticipating potential problems. For example, in a situation where two schools with falling rolls had been recently reorganised into one, the head asked staff for concerns statements about their 'new' building before their first meeting and at periodic intervals during the school year. These statements then became the basis for staff discussions of how they were feeling, how things were going and how they might handle specific problems. Thus, the statements contributed significantly to the establishment of productive, positive professional relationships.

A somewhat different application of CBAM is that practised by a staff developer who provides SoC and LoU training to those teachers who serve as INSET leaders, helping teachers or team leaders. In addition, these teachers are instructed in the techniques of the one-legged conference, and how it can be used to identify individuals' concerns and levels of use. By giving them a concrete, flexible and accurate assessment tool, the training helps these peer leaders to understand more precisely what needs their colleagues are expressing. At the same time, it ensures that they share a common language both with fellow teacher-facilitators and with external resource people, which can enhance communication and encourage productive consultation.

Summative Evaluation

After an innovation has been in use for a substantial period of time and implementation has sufficiently progressed, questions of outcome assume paramount importance. As I have tried to stress throughout this volume, premature emphasis on outcomes can have damaging effects on an innovation in progress, and in any case is unlikely to be of much practical value, since there would not have been time for any meaningful results to be produced.

But at a certain point it is only natural to question what has and has not been accomplished with an innovation. It may be extremely useful, as well. Some objective demonstration of the tangible results achieved will certainly be of interest to LEAs, and may in fact be required by central government as a prerequisite to continued funding. At the same time, such summative evaluation has considerable internal value to the school as a means of gauging the most appropriate next steps to take with the innovation, guiding the allocation of existing funds and also learning from the inevitable mistakes. Finally, summative evaluation is important as a means of determining whether or not institutionalisation has been achieved which, as we have seen, constitutes the final criterion for innovation continuance.

In attempting to evaluate an innovation's outcomes, we will inevitably also turn our attention back to whatever goals were set before initiation began. Having already served as a target to aim for, they can now be used as an objective referrent against which to measure the results actually achieved. Even if no goals were initially set, the three diagnostic dimensions of CBAM can still be used, of course, to assemble an objective picture of how things stand with the innovation at the present time. In either case, the value of such evaluation data will be greatly increased if a preliminary assessment of staff concerns and levels and patterns of use was undertaken early on in the course of the innovation, so that actual outcomes can be measured not only against the anticipated results, but also against baseline data.

It should also be noted that even the most carefully elaborated, enthusiastically supported and assiduously pursued goals will not necessarily be achieved. Even if all the other pitfalls are avoided, and they are legion, one of the most persistent yet elusive characteristics of change is its unpredictability, particularly with regard to outcomes. Indeed, if there can be anything approaching certainty concerning an innovation, it is that it will produce some utterly unanticipated results. These are not necessarily negative, though they may be; but in either case they well may involve some fundamental changes in perspective which can significantly influence the original goals. Thus, even, or especially, in the case of a successfully implemented programme, the learning and inspiration it has sparked may have enabled things

135

to proceed far beyond the point originally visualised. The point is that goals are no more absolute
than any other component or dimension of the change
process; rather, they are a potentially valuable
tool to be used as occasion and experience warrant,
and to be put aside when their usefulness has been
outlived. But even if they are eventually sur-
passed, they still can tell us a great deal about
the course of our innovation effort that is relevant
and helpful.

There are many ways that the dimensions of CBAM
can be applied to summative evaluation, and, before
choosing which tools to use, practitioners may find
it helpful to ask themselves the following questions: what aspect(s) of teacher or innovation
change am I interested in assessing? what degree of
rigour is needed? how much time and expense do I
have to invest in training and data collection?
from how many people do I need to collect data? The
answers to these questions will be determined in
part by the purpose of the evaluation; a formal
evaluation undertaken for research purposes, for
example, will obviously require more 'psychometric
rigour' than a less ambitious assessment intended
purely for internal guidance. This distinction, in
turn, may have a lot to do with choosing the CBAM
tools to use. The Stages of Concern Questionnaire
(SoCQ), the Levels of Use Interview and the Innovation Configuration Checklists are those most valid
for research purposes; at the same time, they are
the most time-consuming approaches. Open-Ended
Concerns Statements and one-legged conferences are
less rigorous but also less time-consuming, and can
provide brief but valuable assessments. On the
other hand, the SoCQ takes less time to score than
do the open-ended statements; this may become a
factor when the concerns of more than thirty people
need to be assessed.

Population size is also a consideration in
connection with LoU and IC interviews, which have to
be conducted face-to-face. If it is not possible to
interview everyone, a minimum sample of 10 per cent,
preferably 20 per cent, may be used. Samples may be
random or may be representative of years of
experience with the innovation or other criteria,
depending once again on the data's anticipated use.
And of course, if one-legged conferences are used
instead of the more formal interviews, even more
time can be saved.

With SoCQ data there is rarely any need for
sampling, since it can be scored by computer; thus

it is usually possible to collect concerns data from the entire population, even when use data must be more limited. When collecting written data, we have found certain procedures to be particularly useful. First, teachers should be clearly and fully informed about what the data will be used for and who will have access to it; this small courtesy can go a long way to increasing cooperation. At the same time, appropriate steps can be taken to ensure that everyone understands what 'the innovation' is that is being assessed. Second, allow sufficient time for completion of the questionnaire or open-ended statement. In a staff or department meeting, 15-20 minutes should suffice. In the interests of confidentiality, it may help to provide teachers with envelopes in which they can seal the written data before handing it in. Alternatively, reference numbers might be used instead of names. This protects privacy while still allowing written and interview data to be matched with other data collected at different times during the school year. Finally, an easy and effective way to increase the return rate for questionnaires mailed to teachers is to post them a week before LoU interviews are scheduled, and to collect them at the interviews.

Thus, in one or another application, the CBAM diagnostic dimensions can be useful at every point in the change process. Because of their complementarity and flexibility, they are able to respond to a wide variety of specific needs and situations. Ultimately, however, they all are limited by their essentially diagnostic nature: they can describe, but they can not follow through; they can help pinpoint problems, but they can not effect solutions. To do this, a fundamentally different type of activity is called for; one that requires far more active involvement on the part of the head or other change facilitator. It is this prescriptive dimension of CBAM to which we now turn.

INTERVENTIONS

Throughout our discussion of SoC, LoU and IC repeated reference has been made to the change facilitator (CF). This person's importance to the change process has been suggested, if only by the frequency of mention; but there has been little or no direct indication of just who this person is, and what is the nature of the role she or he fills. To some extent, this reticence has been deliberate. To begin with, this book is primarily concerned with evaluation of practice, not prescriptive behaviour; and in any case, the concept of active intervention in classroom activities by heads or outside agents is a potentially delicate one and also one that travels perhaps less readily across national and cultural lines. These considerable caveats notwithstanding, however, at a certain point it becomes difficult if not impossible to talk about the descriptive measurement of change efforts without making reference to more active, prescriptive involvement. Indeed, the implicit fact that ties together the various CBAM applications we have just discussed is precisely the CF's involvement and activity on behalf of the attempted innovation. This is particularly true with respect to our second general area of applications, supporting change; but to some extent it applies to the others, as well. We will have more to say about leadership, per se, and the organisational and structural forms it may take, in a subsequent section; for the moment, though, it is sufficient to stress the importance of action in support of change, and to proceed with an examination of how that action may be understood within the total CBAM framework.

Interventions, then, are in one sense the logical result of the other three dimensions of CBAM. SoC, LoU and IC are tools, after all, and tools imply a user. Diagnosis may undoubtedly be considered a legitimate end in its own right, by researchers, at any rate; but from a practitioner's viewpoint, diagnosis that does not lead swiftly and certainly to some productive action is a luxury few can afford. As we have seen, however, merely supplying heads with additional information about their schools, or the descriptive tools with which they can acquire it themselves, does not necessarily point the way to action. Just as teachers need to be concretely illuminated regarding what to do with an innovation in order to reduce concerns, improve use and enhance or extend innovation configuration, so facilitators, too, need something to assist them in making timely, effective interventions. Indeed, for those heads more accustomed to administration and management tasks than to direct involvement in innovation efforts, and, for that matter, for teachers more accustomed to classroom autonomy than to monitoring, interviews and periodic evaluation, the very word 'intervention' may seem somewhat sinister and threatening.

But these apprehensions are unfounded, as a closer look at the concept of interventions will quickly show. As we have seen, both SoC and LoU, and to a lesser extent IC as well, focus primarily on the needs of individual teachers. And since it is precisely these descriptive dimensions that form the basis for the design and delivery of interventions, the resulting behaviours will in most cases be welcomed by recipients, who will be greatly relieved to be receiving such appropriate and timely aid. As far as heads are concerned, interventions in a sense represent merely a more systematic and coordinated version of the accountability that is increasingly being required of them, with the added advantages of greater coherence and clarity. Thus, far from making more work for them, these behaviours, once understood and assimilated, are actually ways both to save time and maximise the practical effects of time spent. Within the overall CBAM umbrella, interventions are conceptualised in two different ways; taken together, they effectively describe the full range of intervention activity from a practitioner's viewpoint. Perhaps the best way to grasp that viewpoint, then, is simply to examine them in turn.

Intervention Taxonomy
Obviously, before any productive action can be taken, the nature of that action must be understood. It is also extremely helpful for the would-be change facilitator to understand the range of potential facilitative behaviours, since this expands the possibilities for effective involvement. These are precisely the needs met by the intervention taxonomy, which provides a comprehensive picture of the different levels of interventions and their interlocking, hierarchical nature (Hall & Hord, 1984).
Interventions, as CBAM defined, are <u>actions or events, taken singly or in sets, that influence the use of an innovation</u> (Hall & Hord, 1984). The generality of this definition is a tacit acknowledgement of the incredibly broad range of diverse forms interventions may take. In fact, it has taken CBAM researchers years of field work to arrive at even this relatively stable working definition, that seems to encompass all or most of what our investigations of change efforts in actual schools have revealed about the behaviour of CFs in connection with innovation efforts. Even so, the definition says nothing about the nature of the intervention's

effects, their magnitude or number. Nor does it concern itself with specific characteristics of the innovation itself, or of the facilitator's style. It is simply a broad, generic category of change-related behaviour.

Within the Intervention Taxonomy (IT), these behaviours are classified according to six levels: policy, master plan, master plan component, strategy, tactic and incident. Each level represents a different kind of behaviour; they are distinguished from one another by, among other things, considerations of scope, duration, and number of users affected. Taken together, they form an array expressing the full range of magnitude, impact and intensity of the various types of facilitative, or nonfacilitative, behaviour.

Policies. The broadest possible interventions are policies. These are comprehensive decisions governing patterns of behaviour within a school or other institution. They may be internally or externally made; in either case, they influence overall organisational behaviour, and thus their effects are not specific to a particular innovation. Policies may be formal or informal; the former are usually written and are in any case established, objective formulations that are known and understood by organisation members and are generally backed by some formal authority. Informal policies, on the other hand, are not written down and may not be understood or accepted by all members of the organisation. Violation of an informal policy is more likely to result in peer disapproval than in formal sanctions. They can, however, be equally influential in shaping an innovation or its implementation. Also, since policies are usually in place for an extended period of time, they often represent a stable backdrop against which a change may proceed. If, for example, an LEA has a policy that spells out conditions under which teachers can or cannot attend INSET, it would obviously affect any innovation-related INSET plans.

Master Plan. The next level of intervention is the master plan; unlike policies, master plans are innovation specific. A master plan consists of all the interventions associated with a particular change effort, whether workshops, individual consultation, peer observation, monitoring, or what have

you. Ideally, the master plan would be specified
before implementation was begun, as part of the
advance planning; in practice, however, this is
often not the case, either because there is no
comprehensive advance planning or because the
overall approach to the innovation undergoes major
change in the course of implementation. In many
cases, therefore, a complete and accurate master
plan can only be elaborated after the fact. Either
way, a master plan provides a map of all actions
taken, or to be taken, that influence adoption,
implementation and use of an innovation in a given
setting.

Master Plan Components. Perhaps the most important
intervention level for most practitioners is the
master plan component. At this level, the various
kinds of interventions included in the master plan
are grouped under six main components, each representing a basic functional cluster of behaviours.
Examples of master plan components would include
training, monitoring, and consultation. The significance of this level for facilitators is that it
helps them to think in terms of the major parts of a
master plan, and to recognise what each part entails
or requires. Thus it is a key to the difficult
transition from theory to practice, and to ensuring
that something like the theory does indeed become
practice. It is worth noting that, although the six
master plan components represent common basic types
of interventions, not all of them will necessarily
be included in a given innovation effort, either
owing to some lack in the master plan design or
because of inappropriateness to the specific innovation in question. Even by their absence, however,
the master plan components may have something to
tell us; if there are no interventions in a given
category, it could suggest either a lack of attention on the part of the facilitator(s) or a limita-
tion in the scope and/or effectiveness of the
innovation itself. I will have a good deal more to
say about the master plan components, and their
meaning for facilitators, subsequently.
     The three remaining intervention levels are
more limited in scope, being tailored to increasingly specific innovation-related objectives. They are
all, in a sense, subsets of master plan components,
and are distinguished from one another principally
on the basis of duration.

Strategies. The first of these are strategies, relatively long-term sets of objectives for the innovation. They represent the translation of the various master plan components into yet more specific groups of actions carried out over time and designed to accomplish particular purposes; for practitioners, in other words, strategies are a way of looking ahead over the course of the coming school year and anticipating the types of actions that will need to be taken with respect to an innovation. Interventions carried out within a given strategy will thus have continuity and be geared to a particular topic or innovation task. It is also at this level that the assumptions and philosophies of individual CFs will begin to have an impact. Variables such as the timing of INSET, for example, could be affected by the CF's approach to and understanding of the change process. A facilitator using CBAM might plan training modules in response to individuals' developing Stages of Concern and Levels of Use, whereas a facilitator following an Organisational Development model would be likely to target interventions at groups of users, emphasising group process skills in INSET sessions.

Tactics. The next level of interventions, tactics, are the subparts of strategies; a cluster of coordinated tactics generally constitutes a strategy. As major operational units of the master plan, tactics are critically important on a day-to-day basis. They tend to be targeted toward all or most of the prospective users of an innovation, and to take anything from a few hours to several days. They are, therefore, very much a part of the fabric of the normal working day, unlike the other, longer term levels. Typical tactics include workshops, meetings and any series of repeated small-scale actions, such as a regularly issued newsletter.

Incidents. The smallest level of interventions, and probably the most overlooked, is incidents. They are the very short-term, day-to-day interactions that constitute the basic 'stuff' of a head or CF's daily work. An incident may take place between individuals, as a face-to-face interaction, or may entail the delivery of a single action to many individuals at the same time, such as a memo from the CF to teachers. They are, in fact, constantly occurring, and their very ubiquitousness may have contributed to their general 'invisibility' to change researchers and practitioners alike.

Research has shown, however, that incident interventions are critical both to understanding the change process, whether at the time they occur or in retrospect, and to the achievement of successful implementation. Taken individually, most incident interventions have minimal effects; but their numbers are so large that they cumulatively assume enormous influence over an innovation. In a study of nine elementary school principals in the USA, for example, nearly two thousand incident interventions were documented during a single school year, in connection with the implementation of relatively simple curriculum innovations (Hord & Huling-Austin, 1986).

Implications of IT. What, then, does all of this mean for practitioners? Essentially, the intervention framework provides a way of visualising what the facilitator does or has done or might do with respect to an innovation. The different levels represent successive contexts within which facilitative behaviour takes place; their hierarchical, interlocking nature points up both the multiple ramifications of even a single action, and the complex ways the CF's approach to an innovation, reflected in the kinds of decisions made about organisational arrangements, affects its implementation.

Simply stated, the Intervention Taxonomy stresses two things: <u>the need for long-term planning carried out well in advance</u>, and at the same time, the equally important <u>need to be concerned with short-term behaviours</u>. For facilitators operating on the day-to-day level, it may seem easier to think in terms of <u>objectives</u> (strategies) and <u>enabling activities</u> (tactics and incidents). Within this simplified framework, the functions of the various levels can perhaps more readily be seen. In any case, the most important aspect of IT for facilitators, in terms of maximising the effects of actions taken and improving the prospects for successful implementation, is the master plan components, which therefore require a more detailed examination.

More About Master Plan Components. The real significance of the master plan components is that they
are at once comprehensive enough to permit and
encourage long-range planning, and concrete enough
to relate directly and obviously to the facilitator's customary daily behaviours. The first four
components, in particular, are vitally important in
helping to underscore what most needs to be done to
support and encourage successful innovation.

There are six master plan components, covering
different aspects of the change facilitator's work
with the innovation. The first of these is developing supportive organisational arrangements. This
would include all actions taken to develop policies,
plan, manage staff and funds and deal with logistical and material considerations. Provision of
equipment, materials and space; restructuring of
roles and timetables to accommodate innovation
needs; replanning staff allocations; and allocating
resources would all fall under this category. Some
of these activities would obviously precede
implementation; others would continue throughout the
innovation process.

The second master plan component is training.
It embraces all formal, structural and/or preplanned
actions undertaken to facilitate the development of
positive attitudes, knowledge and skills in those
who will be using the innovation. Training is
usually associated with INSET, workshops and other
organised educational programmes for users; it could
also include modelling or demonstrating the use of
the innovation. It is important to note that
effective training is not a one-shot, short-term
endeavour; rather, it is something that continues
over time, as teachers are beginning to use the
innovation and their specific concerns are emerging.

The third master plan component is providing
consultation and reinforcement. This component
represents the less formal, more specific and more
personalised behaviours that constitute a major part
of the typical school leader's day. The actions
comprising this component are usually problem-
specific and are often targeted at individuals or
small groups, whether users or nonusers. They are
often one-to-one, and include the kind of informal,
brief conversations that constitute much of the
interaction between a head or senior member of staff
and individual staff members. Examples of this kind
of follow-up behaviour include telling a staff
member how well things are going, informal sharing

of tips and information, facilitating a problem-solving group or organising peer support sessions.

The fourth component, <u>monitoring and evaluation</u>, consists of actions taken to discover what is happening with the innovation within the school. It usually entails data collection, whether formal or informal, as well as analysis and reporting. The monitoring component is a way to gain perspective on what has actually been accomplished with the innovation once implementation is under way. It is also a natural complement to consultation/reinforcement, in that it provides valuable data about how individuals are doing and thus, what their specific assistance needs might be. In assessing individuals' innovation use and needs, the other CBAM dimensions, SoC and LoU and IC, would have obvious relevance. Other monitoring/evaluation activities could include administering end-of-workshop questionnaires or formally conferring with teachers to survey how the new programme is going.

These four constitute the heart of the master plan components, since they are internally focused and comprise the bulk of the average school leader's day-to-day activities. There are two additional, externally focused components, however, that address potentially important, if often overlooked aspects of facilitating change. The fifth master plan component, then, is <u>external communication</u>. This includes those actions taken to inform individuals outside the user group about the innovation, and also to gain their support. The targeted individuals or groups might include parents, LEA personnel or teachers in other schools. This kind of behaviour is essentially descriptive in purpose; it simply attempts to convey an accurate picture of what is being done with the innovation. Some examples of external communication would be reports to the LEA or governors, Parents' Evening presentations or a public relations campaign within the community.

A sixth, related master plan component is <u>dissemination</u>. Although there may be some overlap here with MPC 5, the major difference is that dissemination is actively aimed at encouraging others to adopt the innovation, not merely informing them about it.

As noted, the last two components are somewhat secondary, in practice if not in theory. They might be termed desirable but optional behaviours, since their scope and focus lie beyond the school, the arena in which most heads concentrate their energies. This is not to say that they can not be of significant use to a head or other CF as an adjunct to internally focused change facilitation activities. Enlisting the support of parents and LEA officials would have obvious practical advantages, and working to encourage the wider spread of an innovation can lead to highly productive forms of interschool cooperation, whether in sharing of materials and experience or in pooling resources and capabilities. But the fact remains that, for most heads, the school is the primary focus of activity, and there is usually too little time to manage everything that cries out for attention even within that somewhat narrow realm, much less to look beyond it.

The first four, or 'core' master plan components, however, will be immediately familiar to every school leader, whether in theory or practice, directly or indirectly, because they all pertain to the kinds of things that school leaders do (or wish they had time to do), or at least need to think about, in the course of their daily work. In this sense, they do not represent anything new; rather, it is a question of attention, of emphasis. Traditionally, in the USA, equipment and materials have been supplied to teachers for their innovation use; teachers have been provided with training, too. Unfortunately, this has too often consisted of two days of INSET before the school year begins, after which each teacher is given a ceremonial pat on the back and told, 'Now, go out and do it!' As we now know, however, and as this book has attempted to illustrate, effective training must be spaced out over time, and designed to meet teachers' developing and shifting concerns as the change process unfolds. Happily in the UK there has recently been increased central funding for INSET, for what are called 'long courses': a minimum of twenty days, often as long as ten consecutive weeks. Four priority areas were designated in 1983, the first year, rising to fourteen in 1986 with a corresponding increase in funding. From April 1987, central government has taken over the allocation of all INSET funding, ranging from one day courses to one year diploma and higher degree sabbaticals, under the Grant Related InService Training Scheme (GRIST). There is plainly not only a governmental emphasis on INSET, but a determination that there be accountability over the ways in which it is carried out.

But even this is not enough. Unless components three and four are also actively pursued, equipment will sit unused and INSET serve no purpose. Unfortunately, consultation, monitoring and evaluation have in the past been critically neglected. And, as an impressive and ever-growing body of research has shown, it is precisely these functions that will ultimately make or break an implementation effort, and thus decide the innovation's fate in the school. Their practical importance, then, cannot be overestimated. And for the school leader, it is essential to remember two things: first, that all the master plan components, like the other dimensions of CBAM, are activities continuing over a considerable period of time; and secondly, that vital as they are to successful implementation and institutionalisation, they cannot be expected to develop spontaneously or without special effort. Although many of the components focus specifically on teachers, it must be clearly recognised that, for the most part, teachers cannot or will not attend to them on their own. Thus, once again, we are confronted with the need for a strong on-site change facilitator, who can oversee the evolving innovation process and ensure that all vital innovation aspects and user needs are considered. In addition to the various levels of the Intervention Taxonomy, there is a second CBAM tool to help guide CFs through the complex business of overseeing change.

Intervention Anatomy

I have already summarised the fundamental message of IT in two main points: the need for long-term, advance planning, and the need to be concerned with short-term behaviours. Although the different levels of IT could be said to address both those needs, the overall perspective they provide is weighted heavily toward the former; by its very nature, the hierarchy of levels tends to subordinate the incident and tactic interventions within the overall intervention framework. On the one hand, this helps facilitators maintain a comprehensive perspective, by always keeping their ultimate goals in mind; at the same time, it also inevitably draws their attention away from the details of the small-scale interactions that constitute a significant portion of their daily behaviour. The purpose of the Intervention Anatomy, then, is to help CFs focus on these interactions in order both to facilitate their use and maximise their benefit.

The Intervention Anatomy, then, is much narrower in scope, much more specific in its emphasis.

Putting it All Together

Just as individual teachers' concerns, levels and patterns of use are examined in the other CBAM dimensions, the anatomy focuses on <u>individual events</u>. If IT is the 'what' of interventions, this is the 'how'. Accordingly, it focuses not on the range of broad intervention categories, but on <u>the specific actions taken by a particular CF</u>, using an elaborated coding schema to help CFs select, design or analyse interventions depending on their specific needs. The Coding Schema for Interventions (Hord, Hall & Zigarmi, 1980) divides each tactic or incident intervention into six dimensions which, taken together, provide a complete and accurate picture of the event and its purpose. The six dimensions are: source, target, function, medium, flow and location. Although they are essentially self-explanatory, the following brief definitions and examples may help the reader grasp their use.

<u>Source</u>. The logical place to start in analysing an action is, of course, with the question <u>who does it</u>? In a school setting, the source of an innovation-related intervention might be a staff developer, curriculum coordinator, head, teacher or student.

<u>Target</u>. Once we know who does it, the next thing we might wish to learn is <u>who receives it</u>? In other words, toward whom is the intervention directed? Potential intervention targets would be much the same as sources, since this is essentially an interactive phenomenon that could be directed either way. In addition, some interventions have the change process itself as their target. It should also be noted that an intervention may be directed at more than one person or target.

<u>Function</u>. Continuing our logical, analytical sequence, we may next inquire <u>what is the purpose of the intervention</u>? Seven general functions have been identified; the first six of these are identical to the master plan components listed above: developing supportive organisational arrangements, training, providing consultation and reinforcement, monitoring and evaluation, external communication, and dissemination. The two different categories, then, merely represent alternative perspectives on these vital functions. As master plan components, they are viewed as parts of a comprehensive, planned change

148

effort; as intervention functions, they are a means of characterising the specific actions taken or anticipated. The seventh function, impeding, or prohibiting, recognises a potential negative or discouraging effect. As with targets, there may also be multiple functions for a given intervention.

Medium. This is the mode or form of the action; that is, how is the exchange carried out? Within the school, the most common intervention media are face-to-face and written. Other possibilities would include communication by telephone, audio-visual formats, or public media such as newspapers, radio, television or journals.

Flow. The concern of this dimension is with the direction of the action. Flow is closely tied to medium, and is in many instances determined by it. Any written intervention will almost always be one-way since, even if the target responds in kind, it would be only after some delay, and thus would constitute a separate intervention. An exception might be a written questionnaire distributed to teachers to be filled out and returned; in this instance, despite the time gap, the written response would still be part of the original activity. Conversation, on the other hand, is necessarily a mutual endeavour, and verbal interventions, whether face-to-face or telephone, are more likely to be two-way or interactive. This could hold true even if the intervention were directed at a multiple target, such as a CF addressing a group of teachers, provided they had an opportunity to respond.

Location. The final intervention dimension asks simply, where did it take place? Some common examples might be the head's office, the teacher's classroom, the corridors, the teacher's common room, an LEA office or conference room, or a Teachers' Centre.

While the Intervention Anatomy tools may seem self-evident, experience shows that they are often little regarded and used; and that planning and evaluation suffer from their absence. There are two basic applications, either or both of which may prove useful in a given situation.

<u>Preplanning Application</u>. The Intervention Anatomy
can be extremely useful in the preplanning mode,
when the facilitator is mapping out an anticipated
innovation effort. As we have seen, in this application, we are essentially paralleling the function
of the master plan components; in other words, the
different dimensions of the coding schema can help
give the CF ideas about possibilities for designing
and delivering interventions. Breaking even an
apparently simple event down into its component
parts can help clarify what is actually taking
place, thereby encouraging the CF actively to
consider questions such as who the potential intervention targets are, and how they might be reached.
Preplanning, although it takes additional time, can
prove crucial in ensuring that what actually ensues
during implementation is the result of careful
consideration of available options, and not merely
of instinctive, haphazard 'muddling through'.

<u>Post-hoc Analysis</u>. Once initiation and implementa-
tion of an innovation are under way, the Inverven-
tion Anatomy serves a number of important functions.
Heads or other CFs can use it to keep a short but
accurate record of their interventions, which can
then be analysed to help them discover exactly what
it is they are doing. Keeping such records helps
prevent the loss of significant details that might
otherwise be smothered in the crush of each day's
new demands; at the same time, it can assist the CF
in maintaining a broader perspective on the efforts
under way. Are there groups within the user pool
who are being overlooked by the current support
procedures? Are there important facilitative
functions that are being neglected? These are among
the useful questions that a comprehensive, ongoing
intervention record can help the CF answer. Thus,
the Intervention Anatomy helps CFs determine <u>what
else</u> needs to be done, or what needs to be done
next. Perspective is among the most difficult
things to maintain amid the seemingly endless stream
of pressures, challenges and tasks; but it is also
among the most useful to the school leader who is
trying to encourage change.

LEADERSHIP

At this point, we have just about completed our
quick tour of CBAM, its various dimensions and how

they interact with one another and with the innovation process. There is, of course, a great deal more to each of these dimensions; for a head or CF to become adept in the model's use, both training and practice are required. It is hoped, however, that the overview provided here conveys at least a basic idea of what the model is, how it works and what it means in the context of actual school innovation efforts. In our journey through the different subprocesses and aspects of change and their corresponding CBAM components, we have attempted to cover the full spectrum of educational innovation. As we have repeatedly stressed, we do not value theories or abstractions for their own sake; it is only when they prove workable and useful to practitioners in the field that they become worthy of dissemination. And it is precisely the extensive field testing and continued research in support of CBAM that confirm its real worth.

There is one vital aspect of the innovation process to which we have perhaps paid insufficient attention in this discussion, however; and that is leadership. Although we have repeatedly stressed the importance of leadership both to the CBAM model and to the change process overall, we have tended to do so obliquely, talking around it rather than addressing it head on. In part, this reticence is due to the extremely broad range of forms that change leadership may take. Both the identities of the principal actors in facilitating change and the organisational and structural arrangements within which they work can vary widely within different national, regional and even local educational systems. Cultural norms can foster significant differences, and in addition, of course, there is the matter of individual personalities and their resulting leadership styles (Hall, Rutherford, Hord & Huling-Austin, 1984; Kwantes & Rohde, 1982; Leithwood & Montgomery, 1982; Stalhammar, 1984). All of these topics are, regrettably, beyond the scope of the present volume; we point to them in passing, to suggest their importance to the dynamics and outcomes of innovation efforts. Despite all these variables, however, there is still a good deal of common ground with respect to leadership functions; in other words, regardless of how they are done, and by whom, there are certain basic categories of leadership behaviour that will need to be attended to.

Change Facilitating Teams

Any discussion of leadership in whatever field usually focuses almost automatically on the nominal, symbolic head of the organisation. Increasingly, however, it is being acknowledged that leadership, like most areas of large-scale human endeavour, is almost inevitably a joint venture involving the talents and energies of a variety of people inter- acting in many ways, some more visible than others. In education, in particular, the role of the Princi- pal School Leader in school improvement has stimu- lated considerable interest in recent years, world- wide, and there are a number of documents addressing this question (Hopes, 1986; Stego, Gielen, Glatter & Hord, forthcoming; Weindling & Earley, forthcoming). But here, as elsewhere, we are beginning to recognise that the head alone does not, in most cases, single-handedly make change happen. Rather, change facilitation is usually a team effort, with the head or other principal change facilitator performing a coordinating role over the varied but equally important contributions of the other team members.

Formal recognition of the existence of manage- ment teams (Poster, 1976) is a relatively recent phenomenon, and this is even more true in the area of change facilitation. Hall and Hord (1986) have identified, in addition to the head or principal, the Second Change Facilitator (Second CF) (Hord, Stiegelbauer & Hall, 1984), Third CF and External CFs. Working together, all of these people comprise the change facilitating team, an interactive group- ing animated by its own dynamic, based on shared goals and collegial cooperation. It should be noted that the change facilitating team, like so many of the other concepts we have presented here, did not originate in abstract theorising; rather, it repeat- edly appeared in the data collected during field research in schools, persistently demanding both recognition and explication. In practice, the team will not necessarily be visible or even consciously recognised as a separate organisational entity; but it can be identified by tracing the functions it performs.

Despite the widely varying approaches among both researchers and practitioners to educational innovation in general and the role of the school leader in particular, there is a considerable measure of agreement about what constitute essential leadership activities. This is demonstrated by the substantial correspondence among a number of recent studies of leadership functions (Gall, Fielding, Schalock, Charters & Wilczynski, 1984; Gersten & Carnine, 1981; Hall & Hord, 1984), whose results are summarised in Figure 5.1. Allowing for relatively minor differences in terminology, all of these lists correspond reasonably well to the essence of the Intervention Master Plan Components that we have discussed in some detail above.

In comparing different theoretical or analytical systems, however, we soon find that disagreements are more likely to be about the respective roles of particular players within the change facilitation team or, more broadly, the overall innovation effort. Just as the concept of the change facilitation team is itself subject to considerable interpretative variation in practice, and, in any case, is not to be conceived as a rigid or even self-evident entity, the assignment of leadership responsibilities within a change effort might be done in any number of ways. To begin with, the number and nature of available facilitators will vary from school to school and system to system; in addition, other contextual and interpersonal factors can significantly influence the shape or configuration change leadership takes. I will have something more to say about this shortly. For the moment, though, the point is that these differences in role allocation are ultimately secondary. It is the functions themselves that are our primary concern. In the words of one research team represented in the chart, 'Our view is that it is less important <u>who</u> performs the functions in a school than it is to what extent <u>the functions are performed</u>' (Gersten & Carnine, 1981, p. 20).

CONTEXT

In addressing the question of context, we acknowledge that this is potentially an enormous topic, with implications far beyond what we can attempt to explore here. At the same time, the importance of contextual factors to practitioners is too great to allow us in good conscience simply to ignore it altogether. By way of compromise, then, a concept with which most educational practitioners, or practical workers in any field, for that matter, are all too familiar, I will simply attempt to suggest what I lack the space or means to detail.

I have already mentioned several contextual factors that can have a fundamental impact on the

Figure 5.1: Identified Functions for Effective Leadership

Gersten & Carnine (1981) Support Functions	Gall et al. (1984) Instructional Leadership Functions	Hall & Hord (1984) Intervention Game Plan Components	Hall & Hord (1986) Change Facilitating Team Functions
Visible commitment	Priority setting		Sanctioning/ continued back up
Incentive systems	Resource acquisition Institutional policy-making	Developing supportive organisational arrangements	Providing resources
	Training	Training	Training
Technical assistance		Consultation and reinforcement	Technical coaching Reinforcing
Monitoring	Monitoring Assessment	Monitoring and evaluation	Monitoring/ follow up
	External relations	External communication Dissemination	Telling others
Explicit strategies			Approving adaptations
	Compliance Maintenance		Pushing

Adapted from: Hall, G.E., & Hord, S.M. (1986). Configurations of school-based leadership teams. Paper presented at the annual meeting of the American Educational Research Association, San Francisco, California.

nature and shape of an innovation effort. Staff size, staffing patterns and the availability or lack of external assistance will obviously all have considerable bearing on the composition of the change facilitation team. In addition, financial and material limits, time constraints and basic philosophical orientations can significantly influence the way the facilitators go about exercising their leadership functions. And then there are the interpersonal factors, the personalities of individual team members, and the prevailing emotional climate within the school, that will assuredly leave their mark on whatever transpires within those four walls, whether formally recognised or not. These factors are nothing new to experienced practitioners, however, who must take account of them, whether consciously or otherwise, every working day.

At the same time, without in any way playing down the importance of context, it should be remarked that it, too, is essentially a two-way street. Context will obviously influence whatever goes on in the school, including any innovation efforts; and certain contextual factors, at least, will by their nature have a fundamental influence on the course and substance of school change. But we have also seen that, given the same working context, some school leaders have been able to produce far more extensive and productive results than others. Context, therefore, is but one among the constellation of vital concerns for facilitators engaged in supporting and guiding change.

Providing effective leadership for change is a delicate and complex undertaking requiring both a broad-ranging awareness and considerable sensitivity on the part of the facilitator(s). I have done my best at least to suggest the basic challenges and how they can be met. As I have shown, the CBAM model, in its various applications, is a comprehensive diagnostic system that can assist the head or CF through every stage of the innovation process; but beyond this, it also prescribes certain needed or desired modes of action for practitioners engaged in facilitating change to take. Essentially, the model suggests that school leaders would do well to form facilitating teams, and take advantage of the greater flexibility, scope and depth of effort they allow; having done so, heads need to provide active leadership in coordinating team efforts, considering teachers' concerns, and working to improve their school's programmes for students. Taking these as goals, the diagnostic tools and methods can then be

used to help attain them.   And, as complex as the
demands   and   challenges   of   change   leadership   and
guidance undoubtedly are, they can all be reduced,
without too much damage, to one essential concept,
Support, with perhaps, as a little nagging corollary, the sympathetic yet determined nudging that
helps to keep things moving.

REFERENCES

Gall, M.D., Fielding, G., Schalock, D., Charters, Jr., W.W., & Wilczynski, J.M. (1984). Involving the principal in teachers' staff development: Effects on the quality of mathematics instruction in elementary schools. Eugene: Center for Educational Policy and Management, University of Oregon.

Gersten, R., & Carnine, D. (1981). Administrative and supervisory support functions for the implementation of effective educational programs for low income students. Eugene: Center for Educational Policy and Management, University of Oregon.

Hall, G. E. & Hord, S. M. (1984, March). A framework for analyzing what change facilitators do: The intervention taxonomy. Knowledge: Creation Diffusion, Utilization, 5(3), 275-307.

Hall, G.E., & Hord, S.M. (1986). Configurations of school-based leadership teams. Austin: Research and Development Center for Teacher Education, The University of Texas at Austin. Paper presented at the annual meeting of the American Educational Research Association, San Francisco.

Hall, G. E., Rutherford, W. L., Hord, S. M., & Huling, L. L. (1984, February). Effects of three principal styles on school improvement. Educational Leadership, 41(5), 22-29.

Hopes, C. (Ed.) (1986). The school leader and school improvement: Case studies from ten OECD countries. Leuven, Belgium: ACCO.

Hord, S.M. & Hall, G.E. (1986). Institutionalization of innovations: Knowing when you have it and when you don't. Austin: Research and Development Center for Teacher Education, The University of Texas at Austin. Paper presented at the annual meeting of the American Educational Research Association, San Francisco.

Hord, S. M., Hall, G. E. & Zigarmi, P. (1980, April). Anatomy of incident and tactic interventions: Dimensions, design. Austin: Research and Research and Development Center for Teacher Education. The University of Texas at Austin. Paper presented at the annual meeting of the American Educational Research Association, Boston.

Hord, S. M. & Huling-Austin, L. (1986, September). Effective curriculum implementation: Some promising new insights. The Elementary School Journal, 87 (1), 97-115.

Hord, S. M., Stiegelbauer, S. M., & Hall, G. E. (1984, November). How principals work with other change facilitators. Education and Urban Society, 17(1), 89-109.

Kwantes, N. and Rohde, J. (1982). Schooline research in the MAVO-Project: Facilitating styles of internal change agents. An overview of the research design, the conceptual framework and some preliminary results. The Netherlands.

Leithwood, K.A. and Montgomery, D. (1982). The role of the elementary school principal in program improvement. Review of Educational Research, 52 (3), 309-339.

Poster, C. (1976). School decision making. London: Heinemann.

Stalhammar, B. (1984). Rektorsfunktionen i grundskolan vision-verklighet. Uppsala Studies in Education, 22, 275-286.

Stego, E., Gielen, K., Glatter, R., and Hord, S. M. (Eds.) (forthcoming). The role of school leaders in school improvement. Leuven, Belgium: ACCO.

Weindling, D. & Earley, P. (forthcoming). How heads manage change. School Organization, 6.

Part Three

SUMMING UP

Chapter 6

A WORD TO THE WISE

We have almost completed our passage through the innovation maze, hopefully having arrived within sight, at least, of the rewards of successful implementation and institutionalisation. In the course of our exploratory journey, we have surveyed the recent history of educational innovation, touching briefly on some of the most significant developments and trends of the past several decades. We have also attempted a brief overview of some of the most broadly influential theoretical models of change, describing their most salient points and major differences and areas of agreement. In addition, we have examined the diverse components of the change process itself, trying to define both the uniqueness and the interrelatedness of each of them.

In a sense, all of this was done by way of laying groundwork for our central messages to come. It was felt that without at least a minimally adequate background in the relevant developments, it would be difficult to speak meaningfully about the change process in schools, both because of a lack of adequate terminology and because it would be almost impossible for the reader to gain the requisite perspective on the new ideas that were to be presented. And perspective is, after all, one of the most crucial outcomes of any successfully carried out and fully realised learning experience. Educational practice has been ruefully described as overseeing the continual reinvention of the wheel; this may be inevitable as far as succeeding generations are concerned, since on the individual level, at least, there ultimately seems to be no substitute for direct, personal experience. But the human species as a whole is distinguished by its ability to preserve and pass on information, and thereby to permit the possibility of what we perhaps optimistically term progress; and for education as a whole, this may mean that we are <u>not</u> doomed to keep on interminably repeating the mistakes of the past in our attempts to innovate and to improve our schools. At least we hope so.

In any case, as the reader will have seen, I did in this volume attempt to build on the information and perspectives presented in the earlier chapters, using them as a springboard from which to approach our core ideas. In Chapters Four and Five, in particular, we drew on the lessons of the past in the course of our explication of CBAM, its dimensions and their meanings and uses for practitioners. And it is to be hoped that patient readers were rewarded with exactly the kind of immediately applicable, pragmatic and effective concepts and methods they were looking for, the promise of which led them to investigate this volume to begin with.

Nonetheless, even the most carefully prepared argument admits disagreement and, perhaps, rebuttal. In and of itself, this is not a matter of primary concern, since I think the material presented here effectively speaks for itself, both on the page and in the classroom. But one of the things I have been most persistent in advocating is, of course, the need for clarity, and that applies as much to the present volume as to any change facilitator's set of plans or instructions in connection with an innovation. In other words, though I do not in the least object to having my positions challenged, I would prefer that it be done on the basis of what I am truly saying, not what I may have inadvertently implied. It therefore seems worthwhile to undertake a final reinforcement of the primary message, together with some clarification of a few basic points. Confusion, after all, is as ubiquitous and impenetrable as weather, but we may at least attempt a kind of limited, internal 'climate control'.

ONE MORE TIME

If there is one single message that I would most like to convey to the reader, it would be simply that <u>innovation and its successful implementation TAKES TIME</u>. I realise that to repeat this seemingly self-evident statement yet again is to risk irritating or even alienating those readers who have already assimilated it; but I do so, believing firmly that this is a concept of such fundamental importance that it cannot be overemphasised. As even our fast dance through the history of change in schools has amply shown, failure to allow sufficient time for implementation and institutionalisation of innovations has been a major contributor to the problems and mistakes of the past, and all too often it continues to be one today. Indeed, the lack of an adequate long-term perspective seems to be among the most persistent and insidious of contemporary social ills, and one that infects virtually every area of human endeavour.

Some progress has undoubtedly been made, however, at least with respect to educational change. There is growing recognition of the fact that change is a gradual, ongoing process requiring considerable amounts of both time and appropriately focused energy for its successful and lasting implementation. This is perhaps more true in Europe than in North America today; in at least some European countries, there is currently significant evidence suggesting that the extended time perspective has been incorporated into the educational system's administrative and planning structures. In Belgium and The Netherlands, for instance, it has become established practice to allocate ten years for the implementation of broad, large-scale policy aims. This might seem somewhat extravagant, and certainly such temporal largesse will not always be affordable; but in matters of time allocation, it is perhaps preferable to err on the side of excess. In any case, the simple fact of official recognition of the need to allow sufficient time for innovations to take hold can have significant impact on the prospects for successful educational change.

To speak of the amount of time required for implementation and institutionalisation of change is to employ a kind of shorthand, since time by itself will not generally accomplish anything, except, perhaps, decay. Essentially, time is an enabling factor that creates the possibility of effecting change by allocating the requisite temporal space. But the real question is, of course, what is being done with that time? In other words, to say that change takes time is to say that it takes support and a great deal of energy.

In this book, we have seen how the innovation process moves through its successive subdivisions in the course of its ongoing evolution. We have traced the progression from adoption to initiation, which takes time and energy, and then on to implementation, which takes a good deal more. In describing this movement, I have tried to focus the reader's

attention on the specific actions or action se-
quences that change facilitators can or should take
at each point along the change continuum in order to
maintain and direct the progression toward institutionalisation. As we explored the different intervention levels, I attempted to convey to the reader
at least some sense of the diversity and range of
possibilities for interacting with the innovation
process in effective and appropriate ways.

In our discussion of the Intervention Taxonomy,
I emphasised the importance of the Master Plan
Components as the pivotal element mediating between
the facilitator's immediate, concrete, daily tasks
and more generalised, but no less important, long-
range plans. Overseeing the necessary organisa-
tional/logistical arrangements, supplying training
and, especially, making appropriate interventions
and providing timely support are the most vital
contributions CFs can make to encourage an innovation's successful integration into their schools'
curricula. This is another fundamental message that
I cannot overstress.

To assist CFs in carrying out these functions,
I have outlined a comprehensive, interlocking set of
diagnostic tools which can be used to collect data
as a basis for providing meaningful, appropriate
support to individuals as needed. Three of these,
SoC and LoU and IC, focus on the innovation in use,
from the point of view of either the user or the
things used. I have briefly tried to sketch the
major applications of each of these tools at various
stages of an innovation. In addition, I have
described two intervention dimensions, IT and IA,
which can give facilitators more perspective on what
they themselves are doing with respect to the
innovation, in pursuit of the objectives we have
outlined.

With respect to the Master Plan Components, a
further word may be appropriate. When I speak of
monitoring as an important function for CFs, I do
not mean to imply spying on teachers, or passing
judgement on their classroom performance. Rather, I
conceive of it as a supportive, sympathetic expres-
sion of concern for the individual teacher. In this
sense, monitoring is rooted in a desire to know how
things are going for the individual who is engaged
in the challenging and stressful business of adjust-
ing to change. Facilitators monitor teachers'
performance in order to be able to assist them more
effectively in working out their problems with the
innovation. This assertion has been amply confirmed

by the testimonials of teachers who took the head's or principal's appearance in their classroom as a sign of their genuine concern about what was happening both in the school as a whole, and in the classrooms of individual teachers.

Something similar is involved in connection with what has been described as consultation. Here too, I am visualising a nonauthoritarian, collaborative, two-way process in which the consultant and the innovation user attempt to pool their resources, experience and understanding in order to achieve more satisfactory results. Working together, they identify specific problems with the innovation and try to find solutions that will enable it to work better in the classroom and thus be of greater benefit to students. We have preferred 'consultation' to the more widely used 'coaching' precisely in order to stress the interactive, collaborative nature of this activity.

All of these considerations, of course, bring us face to face once more with the need for some person or persons to <u>do</u> the consulting, the monitoring, and all the other interventions that have been said to be necessary. This is another point emphasised throughout this book, and once again the best justification for so much repetition is the firm conviction of the crucial importance of an effective, active facilitator to the successful realisation of any innovation effort, of whatever sort. The use of 'facilitator' rather than 'change agent' throughout this volume is likewise not an accident; I feel that 'facilitator' more adequately expresses the ideal of change as a potentially positive experience for all involved, and of the CF as a provider of assistance, support and respect for teachers engaged in implementing educational innovation.

IN CASE YOU WERE WONDERING

The last remaining task, then, is to undertake a final clarification of my position vis-a-vis a number of important points. I don't wish to be hanged for a sheep if it was actually a goat I poached. The reader will therefore, it is hoped, bear with me as I make a last attempt to set the record straight by stating unequivocally and precisely what it is that I have <u>not</u> been advocating in these pages.

Sources for Change

First of all, I have <u>not</u> meant to imply, suggest or dictate where school change should originate. There are as many possible sources for change as there are individuals engaged in the practice of what we call education, and experience has shown that any one of them can work, within a particular school context. I have seen large-scale, planned change efforts, originating at the national or LEA level, that succeeded very well. If an accurate needs assessment has been taken, and appropriate policies and practices developed that provide a clear mandate for schools and individual teachers to respond to, this kind of centralised planning and decision making can work, provided that it is done sensitively and well. And in situations where extensive, large-scale change is needed quickly, relatively speaking that is, it may in fact prove to be the most efficient route.

By the same token, I have also seen top-down decisions to implement an innovation, taken by the principal or head, that have worked handsomely. The key consideration here is the extent to which the head takes the concerns and needs of teachers into account. An authoritarian, high-handed, unilateral decision to implement an innovation may well prove disastrous; on the other hand, a more collegial, compassionate approach can help ensure that the decision will find genuine acceptance by the teaching staff.

Finally, we have all seen bottom-up change efforts, initiated by teachers, that worked well. One particular advantage of this kind of innovation is that the genuine enthusiasm and commitment of teachers to something they themselves have initiated is virtually assured. But this alone can no more guarantee successful implementation than could either of the other methods. Lacking the requisite assistance and cooperation by the head or LEA, teachers will be severely limited in what they can hope to accomplish, and the innovation's prospects for success will likewise dwindle.

What I am saying, then, is simply that regardless of the source of a change or the strategy chosen for its implementation, SUPPORT IS NECESSARY. Wherever the change originates, it must ultimately filter down to the individual level—that is, to the individual teachers and students who will be using it. And individuals need help, understanding and time, as well as material and logistical support, in order successfully to assimilate change. If teachers are recognised as the most vital components in the innovation enterprise, and accorded the respect that their importance warrants, they will perhaps be more accepting of change. And if they are provided with the requisite support, they will unquestionably be more likely to navigate successfully the shoals and eddies of uncertainty that characterise change, to arrive at a secure level of improved practice.

Fidelity
Another continuing, and sometimes hotly contested, debate in connection with the implementation of innovations concerns the need for strict fidelity to the innovation as designed versus the desirability of allowing teachers scope for experimentation and adaptation based on their experiences with the innovation in their classrooms. Here again, readers will find me sitting squarely on the fence—or rather, standing on the farther side, waiting for the ideological combatants to resolve their differences and come on over. As with the question of source, I am not advocating either position; both can be effective, depending on a variety of factors, and neither one will, by itself, necessarily guarantee success or failure.

One of the key determining factors influencing this decision, of course, must be the precise nature of the innovation in question. Some innovations are, almost by definition, better suited to one or the other approach. A reading programme, for instance, may be highly prescriptive, demanding strict fidelity. But teachers tend to follow it closely because they find that when they do, their students learn very well. Other programmes, on the other hand, may not depend on such strict adherence to a preconceived behaviour pattern. In some cases, teachers may be given just the seed or nucleus of an innovation, and asked to work in a developmental mode with it, experimenting and adapting as they go along. This kind of trial-and-error approach both acknowledges the inevitability of unforeseen elements appearing during implementation and maximises the utilisation of teachers' creative energies as a force for change. If the prospective innovation is fully understood by the facilitator(s) during planning, it should be apparent whether and to what extent its design inclines inherently toward one or the other approach.

Another key consideration with respect to questions of fidelity must be the local school context. Depending on their respective Stages of Concern and Levels of Use, some teachers will be more amenable to a fixed approach, others to a more flexible one. To some, the imposition of rigid restrictions may seem oppressively limiting; to others, the sudden advent of so much 'freedom' may seem unduly threatening. Within a given school, established practice must also be taken into account. Teachers unaccustomed to behaving independently are less likely to feel comfortable when presented with so many choices, and the reverse is also true. Here again, sensitivity combined with detailed first-hand knowledge of prevailing conditions should enable the facilitator or other decision-maker to make appropriate choices.

As far as this book is concerned, however, either option can be viable. I do not particularly advocate either one; but what I do emphatically endorse and recommend is maximal clarity, in either case. This means, first of all, that a specific decision must be made about fidelity, in order to avoid confusion during implementation. Teachers and others involved in the change effort need to know, as precisely as possible, what is expected of them.

For heads, then, this means that these expectations, once determined, must be articulated as clearly as possible. This can be accomplished in a variety of ways in the course of the various interventions and other behaviours carried out during initiation and implementation. As pointed out, the diagnostic tools described in these pages are flexible enough to be adapted to the demands of the specific innovation and setting. The IC Checklist, in particular, can be shaped to reflect the decisions and requirements of each individual situation. If the expectations are for maximum fidelity, a highly detailed checklist can express that. On the other hand, if the expectations are for great variety and ongoing adaptation in the innovation as it is implemented and as it 'lives' in classrooms, then a more open-ended, categorical checklist can reflect that added openness. In addition, a succession of checklists can be used to mark the developmental progress of the innovation as it continues to evolve through use.

Confrontation or Cooperation?

The final area in which I wish to set the record straight concerns the relationship between heads and teachers. Throughout this volume, I have stressed the importance of the school leader as a vital element in the change process. There is no question that a strong, active leader can be invaluable both as a major catalyst for change and as the primary change facilitator and manager. And, as has been also suggested, the lack of a strong leadership role tends to create a power vacuum within the school that can seriously hinder the progress of an innovation effort. But this does not mean that heads must or should function in an autocratic fashion, using the inherent authority of their position to bring teachers into submission. Nor does it necessarily imply confrontations between the two groups. In fact, both of these situations are the exact opposite of what I am advocating, and they are more likely to kill an innovation than to help it succeed.

The issue of teacher/head relations is, of course, a complex one. The school itself is a complicated organisational structure, and within it are large numbers of individuals who must interact in a variety of ways on different levels and in diverse situations. Given all of this, it hardly seems surprising that complications might arise between the personal and professional priorities and preferences of different groups. If anything, such conflicts would appear to be inevitable. In addition, the question of teacher/head relations is one that is particularly subject to cultural differentiation. The relative prerogatives and duties of the two groups may vary considerably from country to country, and this would obviously affect the nature of the relationship between them. In North America, for example, the principal is generally recognised as the overall director and manager of the school, whose responsibilities extend into every area of its operations. In Europe, on the other hand, the general tendency seems much more in the direction of teacher autonomy; that is, the school leader is seen as the school's chief administrator, but the primary responsibility for what actually goes on in the classroom rests with teachers under the direction or with the advice of curriculum coordinators and the needs of department or faculty.

This is something of an oversimplification, of course, as all generalisations are; and certainly there is a great deal of variation on both sides of the Atlantic, both from country to country and school to school. In addition, the whole situation is in a state of flux, as roles and responsibilities are being reassessed in the light of shifting political priorities and increased understanding of the patterns and problems of change. Nevertheless, there is enough common ground in the educational systems of most industrial countries to permit some useful generalising without doing significant damage. And for the purposes of the present discussion, at least, the main point is that a head who assumes an active role in initiating and guiding the change process needs to take account of the professional prerogatives and needs of teachers.

At the same time, however, school leaders by definition have a basic obligation to ensure that their schools maintain the highest possible standards of excellence, both educationally and organisationally. In this sense, it is impossible to separate entirely the school's functions and objectives; thus, the head will necessarily also be concerned with educational improvement. Insofar as we have tried to stress the importance of a team approach to innovation, this kind of overlap of roles may not seem inappropriate; and experience has shown that it is, in fact, characteristic of many schools.

I have spoken above of the value of a broad perspective as an aid both to recognising possibilities and solving problems. And this is precisely the kind of input that school leaders, who are usually less burdened than are teachers with the day-to-day problems of particular students, can provide. In their role as catalysts, heads can be the bringers of new ideas, new visions and new programmes to their schools, serving as liaisons between classroom practitioners and the greater educational community. This potential function also underscores the need for heads to keep informed. Just as physicians, once they have completed their medical training, must make a continual effort to keep abreast of new developments in medicine, so school leaders need to stay in touch with the latest ideas, trends and methods. Today, with the increase in educational research and the correspondingly accelerated pace of change, this is true more than ever before. The effective, active head, then, needs always to be searching for ways to improve the school. It is, in fact, this restless seeking out and asking, 'What is new, what is good, and how will it improve our practice?' that enables the head to

provide the kind of dynamic change leadership that I
am recommending.

In addition to seeking out and introducing new
ideas, however, school leaders face another chal-
lenge that is at least as great. Having brought in
new practices and programmes, heads have a fundamental obligation to be supportive and humane as they
collaborate with teachers in implementing those
innovations and making them work. Indeed, this
'person-centredness' is precisely what the CBAM
tools are all about, which is why I have devoted so
much space to their explication.

Throughout this book, I have tried to stress
the need for collegial, cooperative, humane interaction among all parties as an essential prerequisite
for successful innovation. Thus, to those readers
who may have felt that I was allotting too much
power to school leaders, I can only reiterate that I
do not favour adversarial relationships. The highly
active, initiator-type head I have been promoting
always operates with the school's and the student's
welfare foremost in mind. Whatever pushing, inno-
vating and initiating the head engages in, then,
will be done in the service of these primary goals.
And the same can be said for all the other major
messages. Whether we are looking at innovation
sources, fidelity or teacher concerns, the key
determinant to effective action is the respectful,
balanced and sensitive interaction of all interested
persons. Lacking this, almost any approach will be
bound to encounter major problems; having it, almost
any approach will have a reasonable chance for
success.

In closing, I would like to offer educational
researchers and policy-makers an additional word.
As I stated at the outset, this book was primarily
intended for practitioners, though it is hoped that
it will also find an audience among any and all who
are interested in prospects and practices for
educational innovation. To this end, I have not
included any particular messages for researchers
and/or policy-makers. I do firmly believe, however,
that the principal ideas herein espoused are both
practical and flexible enough to be eminently
applicable to the problems and interests of any
education-related group, whatever their particular
viewpoint. There is an undoubted need for further
study of the innovation process, its assessment and
support, especially during the protracted and
critical implementation period. Some of this work
is even now under way at universities and research

173

centres in many countries, and it is to be hoped that even more will be forthcoming in the years ahead.

In the meantime, though, as I have done my best to emphasise, a great deal has already been learned, which can be used as the basis for informed and effective action in pursuit of better schools. Despite the incredible range of variation among schools, school systems and national or cultural entities, the basic approach I have outlined will be relevant, at least in its broad outlines. And once it has been comprehended and assimilated, it will to a considerable extent suggest its own most appropriate applications to each specific case. To any of the readers who may find this open-ended conclusion untidy or unsatisfying, I tender my apologies; but it is, I feel, ultimately most appropriate both to the protean nature of the innovation process and to the unlimited creative potential of the human spirit. Long live the both of them!

INDEX

Index